Homer C. Pickens

TRACKS ACROSS NEW MEXICO

Copyright © 1980
by
Homer C. Pickens

DEDICATION

In loving memory of Edna Burton Pickens and Homer C. Pickens, our mother and father, and for our children and grandchildren, may they always remember their "Grammy" and "Sugar," true pioneers who had a vision of a better future for us, then went on to bring it to life, we dedicate this edition of *Tracks Across New Mexico*.

Foreword and new photo captions
copyright © 2008 by Homer C. Pickens, Jr.

ISBN-13: 978-0-944383-74-2
ISBN-10: 0-944383-74-2

Library of Congress Control Number: 2008930201

Revised Edition, 2008

High-Lonesome Books
P.O. Box 878
Silver City, New Mexico 88062

ACKNOWLEDGMENTS

We wish to thank our friends and family especially those in Texas and Oklahoma who so kindly searched and found the many old photographs that are used in this publication of *Tracks Across New Mexico*. They were generous with their time and went to great lengths to contribute their recollections of our mother and father. We thank them all and especially our dear cousins, Jean Deffibaugh and Jerry Trollinger from Sherman, Texas and Pauline and Kyle Pickens in Cumby, Texas. To Bill Huey in Tesuque, New Mexico we are also grateful for his help in several ways and for his friendship over many years. To the many archivists and librarians in Santa Fe and Las Cruces, we give our thanks and especially to Melissa Salazar and Sibel Melik at the New Mexico State Records Center and Archives in Santa Fe. Also, many thanks to Austin Hoover, formerly head archivist at New Mexico State University who so kindly helped our father in earlier days to establish the Homer C. Pickens Collection. Finally, we thank Mary Fenton Caldwell of Ponderosa, New Mexico who allowed us the use of the picture of the Old Fenton Rock House, a grand landmark now lost.

ORIGINAL DEDICATION

This book is dedicated to my precious family and my many friends who enjoy the wonders of the great outdoors in New Mexico and the Southwest. The pleasure of visiting and working with the farmers, ranchers, and business people—both great and small—in a state where cattle, sheep, and wildlife roam and graze on private, state, and federal lands is a privilege enjoyed by me and all Americans.

I would like to convey my deepest appreciation and thanks to my many friends—too numerous to name here—who worked with me over the years and gave me support and encouragement as I wrote this book. Max Cabber Jr., our Son-in-law did the art work on the dust jacket for which we are grateful, and a special thanks to Norman Brown. I will always cherish the experiences we've had together. My thanks to all of you.

Homer C. Pickens
January 1980

CONTENTS

Foreword i

Chapter 1 - A New Life in New Mexico 1

Chapter 2 - My Early Days 15

Chapter 3 - Joseph Albert Pickens 25

Chapter 4 - Ben V. Lilly 35

Chapter 5 - Edna Burton Becomes Mrs. Homer Pickens 43

Chapter 6 - Edna Burton Pickens 49

Chapter 7 - Vermejo Park 57

Chapter 8 - Early Days in the Game and Fish Department 61

Chapter 9 - Lion Hunting 69

Chapter 10 - Frank Hibben 75

Chapter 11 - Just Doing My Job 77

Chapter 12 - Trapping and Transplanting Game and Birds 81

Chapter 13 - Law Enforcement 85

Chapter 14 - Smokey The Bear 91

Chapter 15 - Appointment as Director 97

Chapter 16 - Mountain Lion Tramples Pedestrian 101

Chapter 17 - Retirement and More Tracks 115

Chapter 18 - Golden Wedding Anniversary 119

FOREWORD

At their home on Smith Street in Albuquerque, our mother and father settled down into the comfort of a life filled with accomplishments and a family well raised. Over fifty years after coming to New Mexico they were finally able to travel, fish and, importantly, write the book they had always promised. *Tracks Across New Mexico* was an immediate hit and was favorably reviewed by several New Mexico periodicals. The limited edition, published privately, soon sold out.

Homer, ever the innovator, also wrote a popular booklet, *Modern Techniques for Trapping Coyotes and Bobcats*. It was welcomed by trappers throughout the nation and a second printing was equally successful. The demand for Homer's skill and experience conveyed in the booklet is still popular among fur trappers.

At the turn of the century, we realized that New Mexicans, historians and friends continue to seek copies of *Tracks Across New Mexico*. Moreover, children throughout the United States are ever interested in Homer's part in the story of Smokey Bear. Since the deaths of our mother and father we have acquired more information of their early married life and many fascinating old photographs provided by friends and relatives. This information and the photographs greatly add to the enchanting story of their life together.

Nostalgic Memories of an Early New Mexico Family

Not far from Calera, Oklahoma where the dirt road came to a creek, the bridge was out and sitting in a Model T Ford, stuck in the mud, was Homer Pickens and his cousin, Orville. Edna Burton and her girlfriends were driving back from Durant and couldn't go around, so they pulled Homer and Orville out of the mud hole. Later, down the road to Calera, Edna told her girlfriends she sure would like a date with that Homer Pickens.

At that moment, a lasting romance burst into flame. It was 1925 and Homer was just starting his new job as a roughneck in the oil fields of Borger, Texas. Edna was a senior at Calera High School. For two years their love flourished while Homer was expanding his horizons in New Mexico with his half brother, Albert. Distance made their hearts grow fonder and Homer wrote Edna on March 27, 1928 from his lion hunting camp near Tres Piedras:

> ...it is a real outdoor life, with spring it has lots of flowers and green grass, tall pine trees, spruce trees, fir trees and pretty clear brooks running and filled with rainbow trout that I have spent several Sunday evenings fishing for. All of this is in the mountains which now are covered with snow several feet deep, but it will soon melt in the spring sun and be a real paradise until next winter.

Their five year romance made its way from Oklahoma to Texas to California to New Mexico and culminated in their marriage in Phoenix, Arizona. For a time Edna was willing to live at the newly built Tanner apartments in Roswell. But, she was a tough minded young lady and soon moved into the tent with her husband at his hunting camp. When the snow melted that spring they made their way to Vermejo Park where Edna again set up housekeeping in a camp tent. For a while they lived in the luxury of a little cabin in a valley now called Valle Vidal. Clayton Cabin still stands and Homer and Edna's sons, as grown men, have fly fished for New Mexico cutthroat trout in Comanche Creek that runs through the valley.

For years to come Edna said that was the happiest time of their lives. In the midst of the Great Depression they saved money and lived in the most beautiful place on earth. Neither Homer nor Edna knew, at the time, this assignment would help shape the rest of their lives for in the summer of 1930 they met and became friends with Ethel and Elliott Barker.

When Elliott Barker was appointed State Game Warden for the New Mexico Department of Game and Fish, his first hire was Homer Pickens in May 1931. Homer's new job was lion hunter and coyote trapper and, when necessary, law enforcement patrolman, camp cook, horse wrangler, cowboy, trout hatchery helper, fish transplanter and big game conservationist. Transferred to Albuquerque, Homer and Edna arrived just in time for the birth of their first child, Homer Jr. in July 1931. The beaming parents had little time to enjoy Albuquerque. Homer's skill as a lion hunter was in great demand and they soon found themselves in Las Vegas, New Mexico where Homer was successful in

FOREWORD

controlling the lion population. But, in less than a year they were again transferred, this time to Santa Fe where a second boy was born in September 1933.

The two young boys, Homer Jr. and Jack E. Pickens, were their pride and joy. The Pickens family of four lived on San Antonio Street in Santa Fe and life for three year old Homer Jr. became every boy's dream. Hunting and fishing was the exciting by-product of his Dad's work and as soon as the boys could hold a willow limb and put a worm on a hook, they commenced their idyllic life. While the little Pickens boys could look forward to years of outdoor excitement, their father was at the forefront of restoring the game and fish resources for the enjoyment of all New Mexicans.

The *New Mexico Conservationist*, a predecessor of the *New Mexico Magazine*, in its July 1930 issue, summarized the monumental task faced by the Department of Game and Fish:

> Predatory animals are admittedly one of the most serious menaces confronting the game supply in this state today, but the Biological Survey is doing yeomen's work in controlling these destructive species. We have always found the officials in charge of the work in this state to be enthusiastically interested in preservation, and to be willing to lend every possible aid in that direction consistent with the scope of their work.

With Elliott Barker's employment of Homer Pickens, the Department of Game and Fish took an early step in fulfilling New Mexico's responsibility for game and fish preservation. The Department's semiannual report of June 30, 1932 ranked Homer Pickens as the top predatory animal hunter when he took nine mountain lions. The other 15 state hunters took the balance of 10 lions. A year later the Department's annual report showed Homer and his hounds had taken 35 lions, of which 30 were from the Jemez Mountains. Some lions were captured alive for zoos and some were shot. Homer had proven himself to be the top hunter in the state and validated Elliott Barker's selection of him for the job.

Ready for his next challenge, Homer and family were transferred to Silver City. In late 1933, Homer was alerted that he was to have an eastern visitor for the coming months. Soon, tenderfoot Frank Hibben pulled his truck and horse trailer up to the front of the little adobe house where the Pickens family made their home on the outskirts of town. Homer and Frank began a friendship that lasted a lifetime.

Homer had hunted throughout the Gila area primarily in the Black Range and Mogollóns. He was well prepared and excited to meet Frank, to train him in woodsmanship and assist him with his mountain lion research. During his early work in the Gila, Homer located some previously undiscovered Indian cliff dwellings. This discovery grabbed Frank's interest almost as strongly as the upcoming lion hunts. Homer Jr. remembers his father returning home with a pair of Indian sandals found on a ledge at a remote cliff dwelling high in the Mogollón Mountains. The loops and whorls from the toe prints of the long dead owner were clearly visible in the dried mud. Frank welcomed this unique gift from his new friend and hunting companion.

Frank rode the trail with Homer in 1934 and his ground breaking research on the mountain lion was published by the University of New Mexico Press. The 1935 annual report of the Department of Game and Fish stated: "During the period from December 1 through June 30, our lion hunter, Homer Pickens, took twenty-seven lions from a comparatively small area in the Mogollón Mountains… For a 10 month period in fiscal year 1935 Pickens is credited with 30 lions, 12 Bobcats and 3 Coyotes…" This included the period when Frank hunted with Homer, enjoying unparalleled success.

Years later, Dr. Hibben wrote in his *Hunting American Lions*, "Homer Pickens, then state lion hunter of New Mexico, was to be my second teacher after old Ben Lilly. Here was a man who radiated knowledge and good humor. Homer knew more than perhaps any other in the Southwest about lions and was one of the finest companions on the hunt I have ever known."

In Silver City, Homer kept his experienced lion dogs separated from the younger hounds, some still undisciplined and rambunctious. All had their own food pans and Homer Jr. was old enough to help with the chores of caring for the dogs. Homer had recently captured two lion kittens, then about three months old. He kept his captured animals well separated from the dogs for the safety of all concerned. Zoos were always willing to pay well for young mountain lions.

Homer was in the mountains hunting with the older dogs which set the stage for Homer Jr. to have some fun of his own. He was left at

FOREWORD

home, riding a stick horse, wearing his cap pistol, and ready to imitate his father. The hunt began by letting the young dogs out of their pen. Then the boy hunter unlatched the cage and one of the little lions bolted. Down the dirt road in front of the adobe house the young lion ran at full tilt with the young hounds in hot pursuit. Bringing up the rear was a five year old lion hunter headed for certain catastrophe. In less than a hundred yards the young hounds treed the lion on top of a fence post just high enough for it to bloody a few of the hounds' noses. It took only a few more minutes for the yelping dogs to knock the lion off its perch and less time than that for the dogs to finish it off. About then young Homer realized the trouble he'd heaped on himself for five minutes of a unique, exhilarating chase. The punishment was severe. First Edna switched him good and when Homer got home, it was the strap. Although Homer Jr. later shot his share of deer, doves, quail, ducks, pigeons, a few geese and many wild turkeys, he never hunted lions again.

October 1935 saw the arrival of the third boy, Jimmy Burton Pickens. Homer realized with a new baby in the household, quarters better than the adobe house were necessary. Judge George Hay, his wife Joan and young son were temporarily living away from their 6th Street home not far from downtown Silver City. Judge Hay invited Homer and Edna to reside there until their next transfer which was not far distant. A mansion by Pickens' standards, it offered hot running water and indoor plumbing. The Hay home gave comfort to the Pickens family of five and eased Edna's life as Homer continued his work as both lion hunter and game patrolman.

Homer hunted lions throughout the Gila, Mogollón and Black Range and became good friends with many ranchers. He understood the importance of keeping the predators under control. With their permission and most often their encouragement he hunted the Ladder, the Slash, the GOS, the 916 and many other ranches throughout Grant and Catron counties. He often hunted on the Shelley's 916 Ranch. By coincidence Mrs. Shelley and Edna were pregnant and expecting to deliver near the same time in October 1935. Young Tommy Shelley and Jimmy Pickens were born within days of each other in the same hospital in Silver City. Years later they became friends when both attended New Mexico A & M College in Las Cruces. Tommy's father, Edwin Shelley also worked for the Game and Fish Department as the superintendent of the Glenwood Fish Hatchery.

TRACKS ACROSS NEW MEXICO

In October 1935, hunters throughout the state were ready for the opening days of the big game season. The Silver City *Daily Press* of October 4, 1935 described a new approach to patrolling the hunting areas and quoted Homer, "...Pickens, hunter and deputy game warden, believes that the new plan will be more successful and that a better check can be had on hunters, than by means of the checking station method." Less than a month later the *Daily Press* described Deputy Game Warden Pickens presenting two cases before Justice of the Peace George H. Keener involving illegally killed deer. Both perpetrators were found guilty, again the *Daily Press* reported, "...according to Deputy Pickens, who is determined to round up and prosecute all violators...He does not believe in being lenient with hunters who break the law."

Silver City was the home of the famous saddle maker, A. D. "Doc" Seitzler. Doc Seitzler and Homer became good friends as Seitzler was well known for his excellent hounds and was a skilled bear hunter. His artistry in leather work has kept his name alive long after his death. While Homer was living in Silver City, Doc Seitzler made a saddle to his specifications and the job included a tooled leather scabbard and stock cover for his 30-30 rifle. The delivery of the unique saddle and scabbard, an unusually extravagant purchase of one hundred dollars, was a memorable event in the Pickens' household.

The two years in Silver City established Homer as an evenhanded deputy game warden and solidified his reputation as a skilled lion hunter. In January 1935, the *New Mexico Magazine* published an article entitled "Puma Enemy No. 1" by H. Lee Jones and featured a photograph of five full grown mountain lions that were taken by Homer during a two day hunt. These five were part of the nine lions he killed in a single week. Jones wrote that in 26 months Homer had killed 218 lions. This extraordinary accomplishment in addition to his polished demeanor in communicating with the public contributed to his selection for the job of district deputy warden in the Albuquerque District. This was the state's largest and most populated area.

The Albuquerque district extended west to the Arizona border and north to Colorado. The eastern boundary included the eastern slope of the Sangre de Cristo Range, the Pecos, Las Vegas, Mora, Eagle Nest, Cimarron, Philmont Scout Ranch and Vermejo Park Ranch. Managing this large district required Homer to spend much time away from home while sharpening old skills and learning new ones. To top off his new assignment, Homer was still called to take his horse and hounds and go to any part of the state where game and stock were threatened by a mountain lion or stock killing bear.

The Pickens family arrived in Albuquerque in 1936 and a small adobe house without indoor plumbing became home. The boys took their baths in a wash tub in the kitchen with water heated on the stove. The house had a telephone but the boys were too shy to answer it.

The little house on Highland Road on Albuquerque's northeast mesa had an unobstructed view of the Sandia Mountains to the east and the magnificent sunsets to the west. Highland Road no longer exists but in 1936 there were few neighbors and they were beyond walking distance. Homer Jr. started first grade in 1937 at Ranchos de Albuquerque Elementary School on North 4th Street. He rode the school bus over dirt roads with his Spanish American friends and swapped his peanut butter and jelly sandwiches for tortillas and beans. Except for school, life continued to be uninterrupted fun for the three growing boys.

On the last Sunday in October 1938, Homer Jr. was struggling with *The Tale of Peter Rabbit*. Edna was helping him make his first book report that was due the next day to his 2nd grade teacher. Homer, gone as usual, was in the Jemez getting ready for deer season. Five year old Jack and Jimmy, three, were on the floor playing pick-up-sticks. The radio was tuned to Edna's favorite station when a news broadcast interrupted with the frightening announcement of an alien spacecraft landing at Grover's Mill, New Jersey. The shrill voice of the announcer reached the edge of hysteria. Homer Jr. could see uncertainty in his mother's face. She explained that they had to go outside and look at the sky. In the clear, chilly night they could see the Milky Way and hear coyotes barking. In a few minutes Edna's common sense reclaimed the moment and Orson Wells' *War of the Worlds* passed without another ripple in the Pickens' household.

The growing boys soon acquired a menagerie to occupy their time. Sue, one of Homer's best hounds had a litter of 12 lively pups, one of which was Yankee Dan, a descendant of Dub Evans Slash Ranch hounds. By then, all three boys were old enough to do chores. They cared for the chickens, pigs, ducks, rabbits, and ever present milk cow. Most fun of all was a wild burro Homer caught in the Jemez Mountains and brought home to the delight of the boys.

The adobe house on Highland Road had a basement with a dirt floor and when Homer started live-trapping beaver, the basement became the holding pen. When the weather warmed in the spring, the pungent odor of four beavers drifted through the floor to Edna's kitchen causing a crisis in the Pickens family. The boys remember their mother's final words, "...get rid of them and don't bring anymore back!" Homer Jr. went with his father to take the beavers north to Santa Fe and up the Hyde Park road to the point where upper Tesuque Creek crossed the road. In went the beavers. Ten years later, Boy Scouts from Santa Fe's Troop 29 hiked down Tesuque canyon and caught and cooked their dinner of trout from the beaver ponds built by the descendants of those Homer transplanted.

The Department of Game and Fish realized the importance of public relations and took a rudimentary step by obtaining a manual windup Bell and Howell silent 16 mm movie camera. About 1936, Elliott Barker wisely decided that Homer had the potential to learn motion picture photography. The camera with rolls of black and white film, a light meter, projector and an instruction booklet were shipped to Homer. No tutorial accompanied the new equipment so trial and error was the learning method. He studied the slim book of instructions and started out on a cold trail. The camera went with him everywhere and eventually Homer's intuitive nature won out. His first audience was his eager three little boys who had rarely seen a movie much less one shown on their living room wall. The equipment included a film splicer and Homer edited his own film. No telling how many feet of poorly exposed film ended up on the Pickens' cutting room floor. Ultimately with advancement in color photography and constantly improving skill, his work gained notoriety. The public saw motion pictures of abundant outdoor life, hunting, fishing and conservation as never before. Homer had reached another milestone and began a new function for the Department. The field of public relations was in its infancy but Homer was a natural with his magnetic personality and his willingness to go before the public with fascinating commentary and exciting stories accompanying the silent film.

Hundreds of school children across the state watched as trout eggs were fertilized, mountain lions were hunted, big trout were caught, antelope and game birds were trapped and transplanted and bass, crappie and catfish filled the stringers of happy fishermen at Elephant Butte Lake. What started as a clever experiment, Homer perfected and

FOREWORD

won the minds and hearts of residents of the state. In the process, thousands became sportsmen and women who enjoyed New Mexico out of doors and, importantly, obeyed the game laws.

In April 1939, Elliot Barker, State Game Warden, sent a confidential performance evaluation of Homer to the State Game Commission. In his report he wrote:

> Homer Pickens was the first man I hired after I was appointed State Game Warden. He is without a doubt, one of the very best all around game men I have ever known. He has tact and good judgment and he is one of the best, if not the very best lion hunter in the Southwest. He is particularly well suited for the Albuquerque assignment. Pickens has become quite proficient with the motion picture camera with black and white film. He could qualify in a few years for the position of State Game Warden.

Homer and Edna were frugal to a fault. The three towheaded boys were known for their hair cuts that were the product of their dad's skill with a pair of shears. None of the three boys sat in a professional barber's chair before they finished high school. While the rest of the nation was recovering from the Great Depression, the Pickens family of five stepped into the real estate market. District wardens were paid little, yet much more than a lion hunter. Homer and Edna had saved carefully and were finally able to buy their first home.

World War II was three years in the future but new houses were under construction on Pueblo Solano off North 4th Street. From there the boys could walk to Ranchos de Albuquerque School instead of riding the bus. These small brick homes on one acre lots had plenty of room for Homer to keep his horse, dogs, milk cow, a chicken house and several dozen chickens. There was no zoning and every bit of the one acre was used for the happy enjoyment of the Pickens boys. They raised ducks, pheasants, turkeys, pigeons and even had their own worm bed fed with Edna's coffee grounds. Old enough for serious work, Homer imposed rules that required them to hoe the ever present garden that was irrigated from the nearby drain canal.

Neighbors were close and most had children. They ran free across the Rio Grande valley of northern Albuquerque, waiting only for school to be out to decide who would go with Dad to fish the Jemez or Pecos or Gila or Rio Grande or the Canjilon Lakes. The list ran on and on as the boys went to Pecos Baldy Lake, the Brazos Meadows, by horseback to Jenks Cabin to fish the West Fork of the Gila, Willow Creek, the Valle Grande, the San Pedro Parks and the Rio de las Vacas. Even the catfish in Ramah Lake and perch from Bluewater Lake were added to the Pickens' frying pan. For the lucky Pickens boys the list was unending and the fun seemed to go on forever.

On Sunday, December 7, 1941, life changed for the Pickens family and other New Mexicans with the start of World War II. That Christmas, Edna drove all over Albuquerque to find toy helmets as Christmas gifts. The three boys were all touched by the events of December 7th and they gave up playing lion hunter for playing soldier. Homer hooked his horse trailer to his pickup and drove the neighborhood boys along the irrigation ditch bank to collect scrap metal to help the war effort. By then, Homer was approaching 39 years old with a wife and three boys and was not likely to be drafted. As Game Department men were called to their National Guard and Reserve units, many more volunteered for military service or left the Department for defense jobs. Homer's work load grew by leaps and bounds.

With her husband gone much of the time, Edna sometime joked that Homer had his priorities in the right order: his Horse, his Dogs, his Wife and his Kids. No one enjoyed it more than the Pickens boys who got to fish and hunt throughout the state as Homer tried to fill the gap left by the loss of manpower to the war effort.

All the men in the Department who served were exposed to different dangers during the war. Hayden Wiley was badly wounded as a paratrooper when his unit jumped into Holland. Carl Berghoffer also was severely wounded when he went ashore at Iwo Jima as a marine. Buddy Caldwell lost his hearing when the ammunition exploded on a ship where he was a gunner. One of the men who joined the Seabees sent back a picture of a big tractor with a human skull sitting on the front engine compartment. Doug Hayes joined the Army Air Corps and flew bombing missions over Europe with the famous 8th Air Force. Bill Huey, who later became the Director of the Game and Fish Department, also was a gunner on a B-17 bomber over Europe. Ray Bell served in the China Burma India Theater and returned to become the Game Department pilot. Others, like Tom Moody, George

FOREWORD

Anderson, Elmo Traylor and A. J. Garner served bravely then returned to pick up their lives where they left off. Few if any talked about their experiences when the war was over. It seemed to the Pickens boys who had played soldier through the war years that the returning Game Department men wanted only to get back into the beautiful mountains of New Mexico. Years later when Homer Jr. and Jimmy returned after several tours of duty in Vietnam their first wish was to do the same, and they fished together in the high mountains of their home state.

Throughout New Mexico, members of the 200th Coast Artillery had already been called and many were killed or captured at Bataan and Corregidor in the Philippine Islands. Everyone was touched by the losses of so many of these brave men. Lieutenant Colonel Jesse Mechem, older brother of Edwin Mechem who later became governor of New Mexico, was decorated posthumously with the Silver Star for valor in the Pacific. Years later Governor Mechem's son, 1st Lieutenant Jesse Mechem, named for his famous uncle, was killed in action in Vietnam.

Despite his age, Homer always had a youthful appearance. He was lean, and although short in stature, stood straight and sat tall in his saddle. Judge C. M. Botts, chairman of the State Game Commission, came to know Homer well and was a good friend. Judge Botts once told him, "Homer, I don't know why you don't settle down, get married and raise a family." Homer grinned and said, "Judge, I've been married for ten years and have three boys who are home hoeing weeds in the garden." Judge Botts replied, "Well, you'd never know it and you better bring those boys around so I know you didn't make that up." Not long after that, about 1942, Homer Jr. rode horseback with his father and Judge Botts to carry a load of fingerling trout on pack mules into the San Pedro Parks. After the work was done and the cans rinsed out, Judge Botts and Homer Jr. fished one of the best trout streams in the state.

As the boys grew, it came time for the oldest to have his own gun. The first was a single shot .22 rifle and then came a single shot 20 gauge shotgun. There were no hunter safety classes in those days but safety came first through Homer's hands-on training. He had a single rule that prevented gun accidents from happening to his three boys. When they were ten years old, they could take rifle or shotgun hunting but only when alone. Homer said that careful boys don't shoot themselves only others. This lesson augured well and the three boys went through life with that lesson firmly in mind. Only when they were well into high school were they permitted to hunt in pairs.

In the meantime, the Pickens boys tilled the family Victory Garden and continued to travel with their Dad. A memorable trip to the Gila fell to the oldest boy. About 1945, Homer Jr. rode horseback to the old Jenks Cabin Fish Hatchery on the West Fork of the Gila River. While Homer surveyed the deer, turkey and forest conditions, Homer Jr. fished for three days. He wore out fly after fly catching Gila trout, some as long as 17 inches. They were fat and beautiful fish but Homer said they wouldn't eat any of them and all were released. In between the Gila trout there were many, equally large Loch Leven, now known as German Brown, and Rainbows. The beauty of the Gila River as the sun set and made short shadows before the canyon turned black is an awesome recollection over sixty years later. When Jimmy was old enough he also made the Gila trip after spending the night at the 916 Ranch with the Shelleys.

When Homer was appointed to the new position of Assistant State Game Warden, there was much celebration among Edna and Homer's friends, especially Homer and Ivahmae Raney. Homer Raney was shop foreman at the Santa Fe Railroad in Albuquerque and Ivahmae was a registered nurse. Ivahmae cared for the Pickens boys as though they were her own. Jimmy was about three years old when the family was returning from fishing at Bluewater Lake. It was dusk and Homer was driving east on Highway 66 at a fast clip when Jimmy managed to open the rear door of the old DeSoto sedan. Out he went, spinning on his head like a top across the pavement. Luckily, Highway 66 was not heavily traveled in 1938. No cars were coming from either direction and when Edna got him back in the car he screamed all the way to Albuquerque. The screams were a hopeful sign but Homer made straight for the Raney home. Ivahmae cleaned and bandaged Jimmy's head and he suffered no ill effects.

At five years old, after a bout with chicken pox, Jack developed sleeping sickness. In a sick bed at the adobe house on Highland Road, Ivahmae cared for him through the crisis. The Raneys were among their dearest friends and the two Homers—Pickens and Raney—hunted together over many years. But, the news of Homer's assignment as Assistant State Game Warden was not mentioned in the presence of their sons. Edna was fond of saying that her three boys had been raised "like little wild Indians," and she didn't want them to brag on their

FOREWORD

father's achievement. In fact, the three Pickens boys had the reputation as the most well mannered game warden's children in the state.

Only one occasion resulted in someone taking strong action against the risk-prone boys. Luther "Bear" Turner was foreman at the Seven Springs Fish Hatchery about 1939 and the Turners had two children about the same age as the Pickens boys. Running free with Larry Jack and Lila Bell Turner was an occasion for most anything to happen. It was good fun throwing Bear Turner's pet cats into Cebolla creek, just upstream from the hatchery's ice pond. The cats were about to go for a second swim when Bear Turner caught the five kids. He "tanned their hide" and told Homer and Edna who doubled the punishment which seemed pretty severe for dampening a few house cats. But, they were Mr. Turner's pride and joy and kept the mice out of the fish food.

Homer and Edna took no chance of being embarrassed by the three playful boys. In the presence of adults, they were always held on a short leash. Family relatives, other than Uncle Albert, were nonexistent in their lives. Texas, Oklahoma and California were just different colored squares on a map to the boys as there was no opportunity for them to know their cousins. In 1938 Homer took his first vacation since joining the Department seven years earlier. He bought a new 2-door Chevrolet sedan as a precaution against Jimmy going out the back door again. In their new car, Homer and Edna took the three boys to Texas and Oklahoma for the first time to show them off. The leash got shorter the farther east they went. Years later, when the Pickens offspring were adults, the yearning for the love of family restored close ties with their Pickens and Burton cousins. And, it was only after the years passed that the siblings realized had it not been for Uncle Albert they would have been raised in the Texas and Oklahoma flat lands far from the mountains and streams of New Mexico.

Uncle Albert was the single factor that contributed to the Pickens boys and later to their little sister, being raised and educated in New Mexico. Albert's encouragement to Homer in 1927 to head west and join him was probably the most influential event that shaped the lives of the Pickens family. It gave them the marvelous life in the outdoors of a young state with pristine rivers and forests when the beauty of New Mexico was at its very best.

Insight into Albert's life also came late. The discovery of his hand penned autobiography and a precious few surviving diaries, photographs and letters revealed an intelligent, well read, perceptive man. With time, a number of books turned up that illuminate his life and extraordinary talent for thinking like the animals he hunted. Above all he was a quiet, private human being who shared little beyond his lovely written expression on the backs of photos and, in pencil, on the pages in his diaries and life story. Only a few letters survived the years. Despite his life as a bachelor mountain man, he was not reclusive. He had many coworkers who became close friends. J. Stokley Ligon, the New Mexico District Supervisor, who hired Albert for the Biological Survey in 1919, became a lifelong friend and his fellow hunters and supervisors held him in high regard. He wrote regularly to his family in Texas and Oklahoma and frequently wrote of his love for his father and mother. But, most importantly, he warmed to his young brother, Homer, and mentored him in a way that produced a leader and visionary in the field of wildlife conservation.

Mr. Ligon faced the problem of keeping experienced hunters and trappers on the Biological Survey payroll. Many were mediocre and seemed to come and go but when he found a good one he moved quickly. Learning that Albert Pickens had moved into the state he wrote and offered him a job. They met in Carrizozo, New Mexico and Mr. Ligon hired Albert straight away.

The National Wildlife Research Center is a facility of the U.S. Department of Agriculture. Its archives keep most of the surviving documents of the Bureau of Biological Survey which was disestablished in 1940. Housed in Fort Collins, Colorado is a treasure of reports, including the years 1919 through 1929, the period of Albert's employment. Among the obscure pages, are hidden the names of Inman, Lilly, Pickens, Ritchie, Royal, Steele, Thompson and many others. Displayed in simple numbers are their salaries and their kills. The focus was clearly on the havoc wreaked by wolves and mountain lions and the ranchers throughout New Mexico were not hesitant to speak out on what the Survey was doing to control them.

These annual reports made it clear that the objective was to exterminate the wolf from the cattle and sheep growers' areas and other locations where domestic stock were at risk. Killing the "last wolf" topped these select government hunters' priorities followed by the control of mountain lions and stock killing bears. The 1920 fiscal year report contends that a force of twenty regular hunters was needed in New Mexico to constantly stay after wolves, mountain lions and bears. Albert had joined that force and within a few years he brought Homer into the group. These early reports of the Biological Survey make interesting historical reading as New Mexico approaches its statehood centennial.

Ninety years ago the Survey used the increase in deer and wild turkey population as evidence it was on the right track by destroying their natural predators. Some of those reports were signed by J. Stokley Ligon, at the time, an authority on wildlife conservation with unequaled credentials. The number of predators taken by government hunters reflected Mr. Ligon's emphasis on their work. His report for the fiscal year ending June 30, 1920 states, "Game animals here have become more numerous, and the stockmen are on record as claiming one of the best calf crops known..."

By 1922, Albert Pickens and Ed Steele were singled out for achievement. Steele took 10 mountain lions and one wolf and Albert took 15 lions and two wolves. The district supervisor also reported a notable event; he wrote for the public record, "Hunters Pickens and Ritchie cleaned wolves from the Slash range of the Evans Brothers..."

G. W. "Dub" Evans, Jr. wrote to Charles Bliss in charge of the New Mexico district of the Biological Survey and his June 7, 1922 letter was made part of the record:

> ...and in reply will simply report that Mr. Pickens just phoned me last night from the Black Mountain Lookout that he had caught the last of the three big wolves that have been on our range. For people that know wolves and the damage they do, and the amount of skill it requires to capture one, the simple fact that Government hunters have cleaned this range of wolves in forty-five days time should be enough said.
>
> We know that this last wolf Mr. Pickens caught has been to several different wolves after they were in the trap and that she has been caught twice before herself, so that will give you an idea of how difficult it was to get her. Mr. Ritchie caught one of these wolves and Mr. Pickens the other two.

Gideon Graham's 1938 book, *Animal Outlaws*, used many pages to describe the exploits of Albert Pickens' lion hunting and wolf trapping. Graham, an articulate, self educated man was raised a cowboy in the late 1800s and early 1900s. He counted, among those whose counsel he sought, Ernest Thompson Seton and "Pawnee Bill" Lillie, but first named was J. A. Pickens. As a member of the Oklahoma Senate for eight years, Graham appealed for the restoration of wildlife and wrote most of the game laws for the state in those early days. He called the steel trap an "Instrument of Torture" and wrote of the bravery of the predatory animals that were hunted and trapped.

As a rancher, he knew the cost to stockmen of uncontrolled wolves and mountain lions. Graham was a traveler and met Dub Evans before he wrote *Animal Outlaws*. His account relates the story of the last wolf killed on the Slash Ranch. The story of Albert catching this wise old female wolf was recounted in greater detail than Dub Evans told in his *Slash Ranch Hounds*. After two other government trappers failed, Mr. Ligon sent Albert to Black Mountain near Beaverhead. Graham provided a detailed account of how Albert, for forty days, studied the trail left by the wolf, listened to her howl at sunset and observed her habits. With talent, observation and analysis worthy of the best homicide detective, Albert laid out a strategy that resulted in the final chapter of wolves on the Slash Ranch.

Graham and the Evans brothers disagreed on one important count. The Evans and many other ranchers, then and today, believe that ranching and wolves are incompatible in the totality. No purpose is now served by debating the merits. Homer, Albert and the other wolf trappers and lion hunters are long since gone and the wolf is making a slow recovery under government protection.

The annual reports of the Biological Survey showed that Albert continued to excel as a trapper and hunter. Each year he was one of the top hunters and in some he bagged more mountain lions than any other. During those successful years, he was assigned to the Gila area where he became a friend of Ben Lilly. Mr. Lilly, by then a legendary hunter of big predators, like Albert, was an employee of the Biological Survey. Many claim the distinction of Mr. Lilly's friendship but evidence indicates that he and Albert were more than passing acquaintances. Neil B. Carmony edited *Ben Lilly's Tales of Bears, Lions and Hounds* and on page 137 is a full page photograph of Ben Lilly and Albert Pickens, each with their favorite dog. Albert's beloved "Nig" stands close and his left hand reaches to touch his favored hound. The picture shows a large mountain lion hanging from a tree between these two famous hunters. Other previously unpublished pictures of

FOREWORD

Ben Lilly were made by Albert and found among his mother's belongings in Cumby, Texas long after her death.

The 1927 annual report reflects Albert's suggestion of teaming a coyote trapper with a lion hunter which proved an innovative and successful strategy against the growing number of coyotes. He was clearly a thinker with native analytical intelligence. By that time, Albert had been promoted to Assistant Leader of the predatory animal control operation for the state.

In the winter of 1927, with Homer as his newly employed helper, they caught seven wolves in the Tres Piedras area. These were the last caught by Albert and Homer. By 1928 the Biological Survey estimated that the presence of wolves in New Mexico was almost at an end. Only two were taken by government hunters that year. Over the ten years Albert was on the government payroll, several photographs he made were used to illustrate the annual reports. The 1929 report featured one of his pictures of two mountain lion kittens he captured and donated to the National Zoo in Washington, D. C.

Tres Piedras had become home for Albert and late in the 1920s he bought adjoining homesteads just north of the largest of the three rock promontories. He built his cabin near a grove of aspen and lived there until 1942. It was there he wrote an insightful and articulate autobiography. The largest of the "tres piedras" is still known as Pickens Rock.

Edna loved her brother-in-law but unlike Homer, was not awed by him. On the occasions of a family visit to Tres Piedras, a short leash was again attached to the collars of the three boys. By 1942, Albert's hard early life caught up with him and he prepared to move to the warmer climate of Hot Springs, New Mexico. Before moving from Tres Piedras, the Pickens family made a final visit to Albert's ranch at Pickens Rock. It was Edna's way to always take Albert a homemade pie or cake and that last visit was no exception. She laid out a picnic lunch with a chocolate pie for dessert. As the boys played, one managed to hit the table and the pie hit the ground upside down in the dirt. Once again the boy's leashes were shortened.

Long after Albert passed away, Homer Jr. visited the old Pickens' ranch at Tres Piedras. Pat Rush told Homer Jr. he remembered, as a very young man, hoping to someday buy Albert's ranch. When the time came, Albert and Pat clinched the deal with a handshake and Albert moved south to Hot Springs. Albert had come a long way from Cross

Timbers, Texas. His dogs Sam and Nig had long since gone ahead to "dog heaven", as Albert referred to the final resting place of his hounds. He had always loved hounds but these two dogs lived with him their entire lives and had covered hundreds of miles in search of the large predators. Albert truly loved them, as he was loved by the Homer Pickens family.

Trappers throughout the state formed the New Mexico Trappers Association in the 1970s. Later the Association established a Trappers Hall of Fame housed in The Kit Carson Home and Museum at Taos. Kit Carson and Ben Lilly were the first and second famous trappers to be inducted. On November 29, 1986, Joseph Albert Pickens (1886-1965) was inducted, as the certificate reflects, "Having met all requirements of the New Mexico Trappers Hall of Fame."

Indeed, Albert met all requirements. He was a talented and generous older brother and teacher for Homer. He patiently taught him camp craft in addition to the artistry of hunting and trapping big and dangerous animals of the American West. From Albert, Homer learned innumerable small but extraordinary tricks of the craft. Coyote poison was a great risk to a lion hunter's dogs. Albert refused to hunt where poison had been used. Albert taught Homer to carry a bag of salt in his chaps pocket. If a dog ate a poison bait, he could quickly force salt into its mouth to cause vomiting and perhaps save its life. Hunting dogs were of great value and, after this extreme treatment, one of Homer's could hardly bark after the salt remedy saved its life but not its voice.

Porcupines were also a risk for the lion hunter. Young dogs found it hard to avoid them. Albert taught Homer to carry a pair of needle nose pliers to pull porcupine quills out of a hound's muzzle. Besides salt and pliers, they carried a couple of baked potatoes, cold, in their saddle bags. With no other food and too far to get back to camp, this was a supper better than none on the trail.

Along the way, Albert taught his younger brother his first lessons in conservation which had been handed down from their grandfather Matthew Pickens. Homer went on to make conservation his life's work culminating with the position of the top game and fish conservationist for New Mexico.

Appointment to the new position of Assistant State Game Warden in 1941 meant another move for the Pickens family. Homer delayed the move by commuting to Santa Fe but a year later the family roots were pulled from Albuquerque where they had grown deep over six years.

FOREWORD

Moving to Santa Fe in the middle of a school year was unsettling for the boys. Leaving their one acre play ground on Pueblo Solano was traumatic but move they did to a small house at 518 Sandia Street. From there the boys would attend Carlos Gilbert Elementary School. A 20 minute walk past the Star Lumber Company and across the big arroyo took them to school. The boys were growing up and change came hard.

Santa Fe offered membership in a new church and a troop of Boy Scouts. Life was different and the boys made friends with children of dignitaries and children who would become dignitaries. There was a daughter of the mayor, another of a judge, and several of businessmen and the sons of men who became heads of departments of state government and businessmen, the "movers and shakers" of Santa Fe and New Mexico government. Neighbors were only a few steps away and well behaved playmates were abundant. Children of school teachers, administrators and businessmen were good influences on the Pickens boys. For the boys who had roamed the state with their father, hunting and fishing, city life and social polish was shockingly new. Raised "like little wild Indians," there was real change ahead. Homer Jr. was nearing the age of social interaction with girls, and Jack and Jimmy had that shortly ahead of them. It was a scary time for the boys.

Homer was growing with his new job. World War II raged on and demands were heavy with so many men in uniform. Homer's travel expanded to include the whole state. Elliott Barker depended heavily on his talents and devotion to his work. Yet, when summer rolled around the boys were ready to travel to the good fishing.

Homer added Boy Scout Troop leader to the demands for his time. In the summer of 1944, he took the scouts on a memorable trip by pickup truck to fish the Rio Cebolla that runs through the Seven Springs Fish Hatchery. Eight boys from Scout Troop 29 along with the two youngest Pickens boys piled into the back of a Game Department pickup truck for the trip to the Jemez Mountains. They camped at the Old Rock House built by Reverend Elijah McLean Fenton who homesteaded in the Rio Cebolla Canyon about 1885. This famous landmark was built of rocks from the canyon about 1899. The Old Rock House, now gone, stood on the hillside overlooking the beautiful valley where beavers had dammed the Cebolla.

These Scouts grew to become notable citizens and Homer significantly contributed to each the concept of wildlife conservation.

TRACKS ACROSS NEW MEXICO

Richard Bradford wrote a classic novel of New Mexico culture, *Red Sky at Morning*, and Bob DeBolt became a prestigious engineer. Bob and his wife, Dorothy, are internationally famous as the parents of 15 adopted, disabled children plus five of their own. The well known book, *19 Steps up the Mountain* highlights their phenomenal life. Dan Peterson became a successful aeronautical engineer, Bob Berntsen a prominent Santa Fean, Louis Rockett a brilliant fishery biologist in Wyoming before his tragic death and Norman Brown a renowned geologist.

The mountain air at the Fenton Rock House was filled with the aroma of Homer cooking trout in his Dutch oven. He had kept his skill as a camp cook and with fried potatoes and onions, frijoles and hot biscuits the happy Boy Scouts slept soundly in the old ten room house. The old Fenton home was a huge beautiful structure and landmark for many years. For nearly a century it withstood time until it was demolished as part of the modernization by the State Parks Division. The Old Rock House along with the beaver dams have been replaced by Fenton Lake State Park.

News of a fourth Pickens child on the horizon caused Homer and Edna to again consider larger quarters and, as Homer always preferred, as far out of town as possible. Colin Neblett, the Senior Federal District Judge at Santa Fe, had been Homer's friend for many years. Judge Neblett was a benevolent man of great stature and firm beliefs. His southern origin was evident in his speech when he told Homer, neither suggesting nor recommending, to go to Tesuque and buy the old Dockweiler Place which was adjacent to his farm. Taking Judge Neblett's advice, Homer did exactly that.

By 1945, the Dockweiler place was over 50 years old. It sat on five and a half acres irrigated from the Tesuque River. Besides the rambling home built of adobe, and nicely finished inside and out, there was a huge barn, chicken coop, workshop and garage, all adobe. East toward the Sangre de Cristo Mountains, beyond the orchard of apple, peach, apricot and plum trees, were miles of uninhabited piñon covered hills. Water for the house was supplied from a well pumped by a real, honest to goodness windmill. The package deal for the old place in the heart of Tesuque was a cool $15,000. Judge Neblett said, "Buy it Homa oh' I'll wring yo' neck."

An article in *The Santa Fe New Mexican* of October 12, 2003 described the historic old home as it appeared a hundred years earlier:

FOREWORD

"October 12, 1903: County Commissioner Arthur Seligman and family were guests at the pretty Dockweiler ranch in the beautiful Tesuque Valley yesterday."

In July 1945, Betty Ann was born. She was the beautiful little girl the family always wanted. She, missed out on the earlier hard years and grew, practically, to adulthood in Tesuque. Although she was spoiled by her big brothers, she grew up outdoor-tough. As a child she had her cat, dog and horse and an occasional lion kitten or bear cub and sometime both at the same time.

In Tesuque, the boys could walk their trap lines from their back door. In the 1940s the bounty for coyotes was five dollars, just right for high school spending money. Jackrabbits were plentiful and dove hunting was a short walk to the Tesuque River, running just below the mesa where the Santa Fe Opera now stands. Occasionally a bear came down from the mountains and turned over the bee hive Homer kept at the far end of the orchard. Homer and boys could have a dog and the family quickly added a milk cow, a horse, chickens and an occasional pig. Jack acquired the Texas Pickens' genes for agriculture and raised quality sheep.

The family called the little blond daughter "Betsy" which became her permanent family name. Formally Betty, she had the good luck to learn to ride a gentle horse named Buck and was forbidden, by Edna, from ever having to milk a cow. She attended school from first grade in Santa Fe without ever having to thumb a ride. When she was old enough to go into town with her big brothers, she was a darling in her Santa Fe Demon letter sweater. To the boys delight, she attracted young women like flies.

Judge Neblett and his wife were perfect neighbors. Mrs. Neblett recently had been released from a Japanese concentration camp and repatriated on the Swedish ship SS Gripsholm. They remained the Pickens' friends for life. The Judge farmed in the southern tradition with terraced land he irrigated. The gophers that burrowed through his landscaped terraces provided young Jimmy a steady income using his gopher traps. Judge Neblett paid Jimmy 25 cents per catch and Jimmy was an industrious trapper. Before his death, Judge Neblett gave Jimmy the .22 rifle he had carried as a boy in Alabama, long before coming to New Mexico.

Both Jack and Jimmy were athletic and loved baseball and basketball. In Tesuque they played with a pick up baseball team they called the Tesuque Tigers and the players tramped out a diamond on a field of the nearby Myrtle Lillian Steadman farm. To continue school where they started in Santa Fe they had to catch a ride into town and return home the same way. Often they stood by the road near the Federal Court House and thumbed a ride home. In those days, they knew most of the people going north to Tesuque. When they were old enough to go to high school they were allowed to ride the school bus. It was a seven mile walk home from Santa Fe and at one time or another, the boys walked it.

Lifelong friends made at Santa Fe High School still remember their visits to the Pickens' home in Tesuque. Even Richard Bradford in his *Red Sky at Morning*, wrote of a main character, cleverly concealed as "Parker Holmes," son of a game warden. College pals recall Santa Fe's fun filled night life.

The Tesuque home was a place where wild animals could come to regain strength, grow and then move on to a better life. And, so it was with Smokey, the famous bear. The story of Smokey has been told many times, and most often told well. Certainly, *Smokey Bear 20252* written by William Clifford Lawter Jr. in 1994 is the definitive work. Credit can be distributed among all who took part in the recovery of the cub, the imaginative way Smokey became an icon and for his long life at the Washington National Zoo. In the early summer of 1950, Smokey came to live with the Pickens family in Tesuque. In preparation for their trip to Washington, D. C., the little bear became accustomed to Homer but it fell to Jack and Jimmy to do the care and feeding.

Smokey made a lasting impression on Jack, Jimmy and Betsy and some of the memories are bittersweet. Jack remembers him as a "mean little critter that would bite you in a second." Homer taught the boys to always wear gloves when handling Smokey because the cub was unpredictable and would snap as fast as a rattlesnake with his sharp little teeth. Jimmy said, "Between the gloves and anticipating attacks by watching Smokey's eyes, I was able to avoid most bites." The boys agreed, even though Smokey was not all that pretty, he was a fun playmate when he was in the right mood. The family's black Labrador retriever was Smokey's preferred playmate but he could change in an instant and once bit as unsuspecting family friend.

It was not unusual for many young animals to be in temporary residence with the Pickens. While Smokey was waiting for his trip to Washington, he had to share the limelight with another cub. Jack recalls a young, light brown female, "She was a pretty little bear and well behaved. Later on, we released her in the Sangre de Cristos." The 16 mm movie film shot by Homer of Smokey living at their Tesuque home tells the story of the little bear's last days in New Mexico. This historic film, now preserved at the State Archives, depicts both cubs, the family dog and Betsy at play before Homer took Smokey to Washington.

In the years that followed Homer taking Smokey to Washington, D. C. the popularity of Smokey Bear continued to grow. The U. S. Forest Service employed imaginative projects to bring Smokey into the lives of school children. One of the most popular is the Smokey Bear hot air balloon. William Chapel was the Forest Service's Assistant Director of Fire Management for the Southwest District. He developed the project and piloted the hot air balloon in major events throughout the United States and Canada. Bill Chapel has estimated that millions of children have seen the Smokey Bear balloon.

The balloon takes the form of the Smokey Bear image and carries the theme of forest fire prevention. In the developmental phase Bill Chapel and Homer became good friends and Homer proved to be a valuable supporter and resource for the hot air balloon project. The balloon has flown at the Super Bowl, Macy's Thanksgiving parade, rodeos and sporting events in nearly every state in the union.

In 1953, as State Game Warden newly designated as Director of the New Mexico Department of Game and Fish, Homer saw an opportunity to raise standards, modernize and enlarge the Department. Some of the men returning from WWII immediately went to college under the GI Bill. Homer knew that education and academic training were imperative to handle the problems that lay ahead. The population was expanding and demand for hunting, fishing and outdoor recreation was increasing. Post-war families were growing and sought the enjoyment found in the mountains, lakes and streams of New Mexico.

Homer set to work to move the department forward. He redefined the game districts and reassigned district wardens. He directed trout hatcheries plant ten inch trout instead of the six inch that had long been the standard. Hunting seasons were lengthened and more frequent doe hunts were allowed to reduce the deer population that were out of control under the old "Bucks Only" standard. Scientifically based studies of many species of fish and wildlife were instituted.

In July 1955, the New Mexico Office of the State Engineer published the Game Department's scientific study, "Fisheries Survey of the Gila and Mimbres River Drainage." The *Journal of Wildlife Management* in April 1956 published a study on Scaled Quail in which the department had provided young birds from the game farm in Carlsbad for Texas A & M College, Department of Wildlife Management.

Homer worked with Dr. William O'Donnell, president of New Mexico A & M College, now New Mexico State University, to build a curriculum that would produce wildlife biologists who could steer the Department into a new era. College graduates soon were hired by the department. Frequently then, and in the future, Homer was recognized as a leader in the conservation field, not only in New Mexico, but throughout the nation. In 1955 he attended the International Association of Game and Fish Commissioners in Montreal, Canada where he presented a paper on Sandhill Cranes. Despite constant harping "to go back to the old ways," Homer continued with the innovations that many saw as necessary steps to move wildlife conservation forward.

Homer was frequently recognized for his outstanding service in the field of conservation and his membership in state, national and international fish and wildlife agencies were numerous. As Director of the Department, he sat as a member of the State Parks Commission and on the State Land Office Advisory Board. In 1957 he was appointed Chairman of the Central Flyway Council; also, in 1957 he was elected vice-president of the Western Association of State Game and Fish Commissioners at their annual meeting at Jackson Hole, Wyoming. The coveted Nash Conservation Award was among the many Homer was awarded.

In the course of Homer's life setbacks were few but politics in the Santa Fe State House can be tricky for a man who came up from oilfield roughneck to coyote trapper, to lion hunter to game warden. Even a visionary conservationist like Homer Pickens, no matter how devoted, can be grist for the mill. In 1958, after five years as Department Director, Governor Edwin Mechem selected members for the State Game Commission that resulted in Homer being forced to give up his position. The governor removed a political liability as an election came on the horizon. For ten years, Homer harbored ill feelings toward the governor until a tragedy befell the Mechem family. Mechem's son, 1st Lieutenant Jesse Mechem was killed in action in Vietnam. At war's end, when Homer's highly decorated sons safely returned from Vietnam his ill feelings towards Ed Mechem dissolved and their friendship returned.

The Pickens family of six made their home in Tesuque for thirteen years. The boys grew to adulthood and went away to college, Betsy became a young woman, and the young Pickens men entered military service, married and had families of their own. The memories of those happy years are still powerful to the four offspring of Homer and Edna. As Edna said after moving from Tesuque, "When we moved, I cried every time we made a trip to the dump, and the memories went on the heap."

The Dockweiler place still stands, remodeled with style and modern conveniences. The adobe barn where Smokey lived and the garage where Edna once killed a rattlesnake with a garden hoe has been turned into a luxury apartment. The orchard has been subdivided and the five and a half acres purchased by Homer and Edna for a pittance has been on the market for nearly a million dollars. In the recollection of the four Pickens children, that is but the price of a single memory.

Little did Homer know how his and Edna's life would be enhanced by the seemingly brutal turn of events and his abrupt departure from the Department of Game and Fish. As though by providence, a new horizon opened for them.

The Atomic Energy Commission at Los Alamos was seeking a conservationist to take charge of their growing wildlife population and fire and safety matters. Homer was a natural and exactly what AEC needed as their conservation specialist. He had hunted lions throughout the Los Alamos area, long before World War II, when it was still a school for boys. Homer and Edna moved to Los Alamos in 1961 and round two of an idyllic life commenced.

Edna always said that one of Homer's strongest traits was adaptability. She was exactly right as he immediately grasped the concept of his new job. Deer and bear regularly encroached on the scientific testing areas. These animals were treated with respect and care. Rather than destroy them they were captured and transported to areas where they could continue to thrive. Under his supervision, wildlife and the population reached a balance in the rare habitat at the home of nuclear research.

Homer and Edna became a respected part of the Los Alamos community. His responsibilities grew as he went about his work with skill and tact. In 1963, an accidental explosion occurred at Medina Base

TRACKS ACROSS NEW MEXICO

Nuclear Storage Facility at San Antonio, Texas. Jimmy Pickens, an Air Force officer, was stationed nearby and experienced the shockwave and saw the massive column of smoke and debris rise in the air. Not long after, Jimmy got a call from his father that he was coming to San Antonio. Homer had been selected to survey the damage created by the explosion to wildlife, trees, plants and drainage. As testament to Homer's knowledge and experience he was selected over scientists and academics to handle this important task.

The Baca Ranch was a neighbor to the Los Alamos community and the ranch was well known by Homer. He and Albert had hunted lions throughout the Valle Grande, Jemez and Frijoles Canyon area in the late 1920s and 1930s. In the years Homer was district warden he patrolled the same area and worked every foot of the famous Baca Ranch in the 1930s and 1940s. Part of Homer's job at the AEC was to know the Los Alamos neighbors. Further good fortune befell Homer when he met James P. "Pat" Dunigan who then owned the vast Baca Land and Cattle Company.

In 1969 Homer retired for a second time after eight years with the Atomic Energy Commission. He and Edna traveled, visited old friends and Homer fly fished the famous rivers of the Rocky Mountains. About a year had passed when Pat Dunigan called Homer and asked his help. They had become good friends and Pat frequently looked to Homer for advice and suggestions in the management of the ranch's wildlife and forests. When Homer was no longer an employee of the government, Pat was interested in more than just advice.

The Baca Ranch encompasses nearly 100,000 acres including the famous Valle Grande with its huge caldera and surrounding mountains. Visitors to the Valle Grande and the caldera believe it is one of the most beautiful sites in New Mexico. Mr. Dunigan knew that the ranch needed a person with skill and knowledge of fish, wildlife and forestry. He asked Homer to assist him in all these matters. This almost became a full time job and Homer and Edna spent many summers and winters living at the ranch monitoring recreational activities, managing big game hunts, controlling predators and the timber harvest. In a letter written December 8, 1977, Mr. Dunigan wrote Homer:

> My sincere thanks to you for your report but most of all for the fine job you always do in connection with our hunt. Your approach is extremely professional and

yet very understanding and compassionate. Please keep in touch and I will look forward to seeing you the first time I am in Albuquerque.

Mr. Dunigan's affection for Homer and his reliance on him was expressed in a letter he wrote in December 1978:

> You know that you and your family have always been welcome on the ranch and I sincerely hope that you will take good care of yourself and that you and Mrs. Pickens will enjoy a very long and happy life. I look forward to seeing you and will undoubtedly call on you for your advice and counsel throughout the years.
>
> I am thinking very strongly on working something out with one of the federal agencies to assure the ultimate preservation of the ranch. I have not resolved which one is best to work with and thought that you and I could get together so that I might have the benefit of your thoughts on this matter.

Pat Dunigan and Homer remained good friends until Pat's untimely death in 1980 but their discussions led to the sale of the Baca Ranch to the United States Government in 1999. In 2000 the U. S. Congress enacted the Valles Caldera Preservation Act. Today the Valles Caldera National Preserve is a uniquely beautiful resource for all Americans.

The pleasure of fishing the East Fork of the Jemez River, the Rio San Antonio and Indian Creek in the Valle Grande had commenced as early as Homer Jr. could remember, about 1938, and the Pickens family enjoyed this great blessing until Homer and Edna passed away.

Homer and Edna had owned a home in Albuquerque since 1959. Although it was for their retirement they had lived in it only intermittently. After retiring from the AEC they settled down in that comfortable home and it was there that Homer with the help of his loyal wife wrote *Tracks Across New Mexico*. Secretary of Natural Resources William S. Huey, retired director of the Department of Game and Fish wrote in *New Mexico Wildlife*:

I can't claim that my recollections of New Mexico go back to 1927, but I do vividly remember the appearance and the feel of many areas described by Pickens. His casual tone and descriptions prompt a visual reconstruction of places such as the Santa Fe Depot and the Alvarado Hotel in Albuquerque, as well as the sensory reconstruction that permits the total experience of having visited that now-destroyed New Mexico landmark. No less vivid is the account of the hell-for-leather pursuit of hunter Roy Snyder's hounds hot on the trail of a mountain lion in the Black Range south of Hermosa.

Years later Bill recalled reading Homer's book, "It was so real I could smell the hot dusty air as they dropped off that mountain top toward the dogs barking in the canyon. It's a tribute to Homer that his words caused you to experience exactly what he wrote."

Homer had few regrets in life although, on occasion, he lamented the intensity of the early hunting of predators like the mountain lion and wolf. He later urged predatory animal control be done at the local level without a broad state wide approach. He said that he was glad to see the mountain lion protected by state game laws and that the danger of lions to humans was exaggerated. He once remarked that he missed hearing the howl of a lobo wolf in the evening deep in the mountains. He probably would be pleased to know that the wolf was making a comeback as long as the wolf population was controlled to protect the ranchers and other stockmen.

Homer and Edna were graced with long, healthy lives and children, grandchildren and great grandchildren. Edna passed away suddenly on December 7, 1985; she was 80 years old and had first come to New Mexico in a covered wagon 1906. She was intelligent and perceptive and sometimes had a hard time putting up with the antics of her daughter and three boys. She loved them unselfishly, evenly and unconditionally as she did her husband of 55 years. She is buried in Fairview Memorial Park in Albuquerque.

Despite the loss of his dearest companion, Homer went on for ten more years of healthy life. By then he was a great grandfather, popular and greatly loved. His full family of 34 includes sons, son-in-law, daughter, daughters-in-law, grandchildren and great grandchildren.

FOREWORD

Homer's 90th birthday was celebrated with a party in Albuquerque and, along with friends and family, Smokey Bear was a special guest. Although the real Smokey died at the National Zoo in 1976, his image and reputation made him a unique icon with his own zip code and website. Covered with brown fur, wearing his trademark hat and jeans and a happy smile on his face, the Smokey icon stands over seven feet tall. With Bill Chapel of the U. S. Forest Service, Smokey walked among friends and the four generations of Pickens' to celebrate Homer's birthday.

Homer joined Edna when he passed away on February 19, 1995 and is buried beside her at Fairview Memorial Park. The family asked Bill Huey to give the eulogy at the funeral. Bill was a friend of the Pickens family for many years and also a neighbor in the Tesuque Valley. Bill spoke fondly of Homer and his life as a wildlife conservationist:

> I was asked by a reporter this week what stood out in my mind about Homer's tenure as Director of the Game and Fish Department. My answer described, as well as I could, the dramatic advancement of scientific game management in New Mexico that he was responsible for. This advancement was recognized by Dr. Ira N. Gabrielson in an evaluation of the Department conducted by the Wildlife Management Institute in 1957. The Institute's report credited Homer with accomplishing the greatest advancement of any western department during the period.
>
> I first met Homer almost 50 years ago. It is not possible to describe all of the things about Homer that have impressed me during that time. Homer was a tough, often times unyielding boss. He wanted dedication to the job but he gave friendship and support to new ideas and approaches that were brought to the Department.
>
> Not only was he administratively tough, he was physically as tough as a boot. I remember reading a field report dating from about the mid-thirties that I ran across in the Department's archives that impressed me with his durability. This report was, I am sure, not an

unusual survey of wildlife and habitat conditions. What sounded unusual to me were the timing and conditions. Homer began this survey by trailering his horses, dogs and camp outfit to the boy's school where Los Alamos now stands. He rode from this point up into and across the Valle Grande, through the La Cueva area, over in the Cebolla Creek on up the Calerveras and over into Telephone Canyon, then across the heart of the Jemez country to Blue Bird Mesa and then back to his truck at the boy's school. This is quite a horse back ride, particularly when you consider that it was done in January.

I have recently reviewed the annual reports of the Department submitted by Homer for his five years as Director. These reports further support the remarkable impact Homer had on New Mexico's wildlife and its wild life professionals.

Homer and Edna raised a terrific family. The accomplishments of their girl and these boys is a further tribute to them both.

Homer Pickens was a remarkable man.

Among the honorary pallbearers were Federal Judge Edwin L. Mechem, Dr. Frank C. Hibben, Retired Director and former Secretary of Natural Resources William S. Huey, A. J. Garner the Assistant Director of the department under Homer, and Homer's close friend and attorney Charles Spann. These friends who were giants in their professions came to honor and say farewell to one of their own.

After the turn of the millennium, with encouragement from brothers and sister, Homer Jr. undertook a search for the historical record left by their mother and father. The old Burton homestead was located near Norton, NM and Edna's history as a very early settler was confirmed by documents and relatives. Her father left the oil fields in Oklahoma when Edna was one year old. In a covered wagon, he took his family to homestead a dry land farm southeast of Tucumcari just below the Caprock. When illness struck they returned to Oklahoma, again by covered wagon. Her early childhood had produced a tough and fearless young woman who was fully capable of dealing with any hardship she and Homer would encounter throughout their long and happy married life.

During his career with the Department of Game and Fish, Homer had exposed untold footage of 16 mm movie film for the Department capturing historic scenes of early New Mexico wildlife. In 2004, the Game Department could find none of it. Homer Jr. finally discovered what remained of this classic film at the New Mexico State Records Center and Archives in Santa Fe. Housed in a large, modern facility, the film was unprocessed and in poor condition. No description of the film existed, only the notation "Fish and Game." The film was wound backward on the reels, broken and repaired with Scotch tape and marked "cannot be shown." For the next three years the archivists and video specialists processed the film while the Pickens family wrote vignettes of the old footage.

When the state archivists completed their work, segments of the film received a federal grant from the National Film Preservation Foundation to restore it in digital format. In October 2007, a premier screening of the digitized film was held in Santa Fe. Lt. Colonel Jimmy Pickens, U. S. Air Force (retired) and Mrs. Betty Ann Pickens Cabber narrated the silent film and provided anecdotal comments. Bill Huey also spoke of the history and contribution made by Homer. Family, friends, historians and colleagues were present to honor Homer Pickens as an accomplished innovator, photographer, visionary and conservationist. The centerpiece film of Smokey Bear and lion hunting in the 1940s remains a classic of the historical photographic record of the Department of Game and Fish and Homer Pickens' unparalleled impact on New Mexico conservation. Access to this rare film is available at the New Mexico Records Center and Archives in Santa Fe.

Homer had a good sense of history and posterity and after retirement from the Atomic Energy Commission he contacted Austin Hoover, then chief archivist at New Mexico State University. The University was eager to accept Homer's personal papers, diaries, books and photographs. The donation was made in increments and following Homer's death, Mr. Hoover took all the remaining material to the archives at Las Cruces. The Homer C. Pickens Collection is available to the public as part of the Rio Grande Historical Collections in the library at New Mexico State University.

The New Mexico Farm and Ranch Heritage Museum, a 47 acre facility, was established in Las Cruces, New Mexico in 1998. This museum preserves the history of farming and ranching in early New Mexico. A. D. "Doc" Seitzler's historic work as a saddle maker from Silver City was highlighted in a special exhibit at the museum in 2007. Seitzler's artistry with leather is well known for its beauty and durability. Among the work on display to the public was the saddle made by Doc Seitzler especially for Homer in 1936. Over sixty years later the Seitzler saddle is still in excellent condition. Homer left his saddle and riding equipment to his beloved daughter, Betsy.

Homer and Edna's grandchildren and great grandchildren are now old enough to be fascinated by their family history. They are learning of the great contribution both made to the preservation of our natural resources and are awed to find the deep respect expressed by others. The story of a brave young couple building a future for themselves and their family in early New Mexico is endearing to the Pickens offspring who are now scattered throughout the world. In its way, it conveys their rugged origin and heritage. For Edna and Homer's children it brings back sweet memories of a childhood, if not perfect, as close as it comes.

Homer C. Pickens, Jr.
Augusta, GA

Jack E. Pickens
Charlotte, NC

Jimmy Burton Pickens
Abilene, TX

Betty Ann Pickens Cabber
Estancia, NM

The engagement picture of Edna Nome Burton and Homer C. Pickens made in Durant, Oklahoma about 1926. They were married in Phoenix, Arizona on January 7, 1930 and had their honeymoon at Vermejo Park until the snow started to fall later that year.

Edna Burton Pickens soon after her marriage to Homer in 1930. Their marriage lasted 55 years until her death in 1985.

Homer's second lion, killed on June 30, 1927 near Gallina and the San Pedro Parks. He had been in New Mexico less than two months and was still wearing his oilers cap and brogans. In two years time, he would be toughened up, westernized and lean from camp grub.

Homer with Skip at the old Forest Service Ranger Station at Tres Piedras about 1929. Pickens Rock rises into the horizon behind the Ranger Station. Homer was 26 years old when this photo was made and had been well trained by Albert for two years.

Homer killed this very large mountain lion in the fall of 1931 in Frijoles Canyon near Los Alamos. Homer Jr. was about 6 months old when Homer made the photograph. It appeared in the October 1932 issue of the *New Mexico Magazine* in an article by Harry Shuart, the managing editor.

Albert Pickens killed this large mountain lion in Cochiti Canyon near the Cochiti Indian Pueblo about 1928. He trained the Indian pony to stand still with the large predator, a natural enemy, on its back.

Albert captured these two mountain lion kittens in Cochiti Canyon south of Los Alamos, NM in 1927. He sent this photo to his family in Cumby, Texas and wrote on the back, "Mountain lion kittens chained in camp but was later sent to Washington, D. C. alive." The kittens were placed in the National Zoo. This photo appeared in the U. S. Biological Survey Annual Report for 1928-1929.

Pictured is a large female wolf trapped on the Evans' Slash Ranch near Beaverhead, NM. After Albert made the picture, he sent it to his father in Cumby, TX. J. Stokley Ligon, predatory animal inspector, wrote in the Biological Survey Annual Report for 1919, "It is a practical impossibility to prevent increase, so long as there is a pair of wolves at large, although they may be old, minus toes or entire feet, or carry wounds made by bullets. Such afflictions have no serious bearing on prolific reproduction…"

Ben Lilly with J. B. "Jack" Thompson and their hounds. This photograph may have been made by J. Stokley Ligon or by Albert Pickens at some time in the 1920s. Albert sent the original print to his mother in Cumby, Texas. Albert's employment with the Biological Survey began when Mr. Ligon hired him in 1919. He worked with Mr. Lilly and they became friends. Later when Homer was assigned to the Silver City area, he and Mr. Lilly also became friends.

This rare photo of Ben Lilly and Albert Pickens shows these famous men, each with one of their best companions. Albert's left hand reaches for Nig while he wears his ever present wide brimmed cowboy hat. Both men are slight in stature which belies their physical strength, endurance and courage. Albert met Ben Lilly about 1919 when both worked as hunters for the U. S. Biological Survey. Photo courtesy Manuel Gutierrez.

Ben Lilly takes his dinner out of doors, as was his habit. Albert sent this original photograph to his mother and father in Cumby, Texas. The date or place this candid image was made is not known and no note or letter survived the years. Albert probably made this photograph before he retired in 1929. He had often hunted with Lilly in the years they worked together for the Biological Survey.

Albert often took pictures of his two best wolf and lion hunting dogs. These two hounds traveled with him for many years. We do not know when they passed on but with certainty it was a very sad day for Albert. He sent this picture to his mother and father in Cumby, Texas and on the back he wrote, "Sam and Nig always awake. Surely if there is a dog heaven I will see them there one day God willing."

The town of Tres Piedras as it appeared in the mid-1920s. The water tower stands beside the narrow gauge tracks of the D&RGW Railroad. This spur was known as the "Chili Line" because it carried fresh chili north from Santa Fe to Antonito, CO. Homer and Albert occasionally rode the train to Santa Fe and back. Pickens Rock is on the horizon, prominent in the center of the picture. The original photograph hung on the wall of the home of Mr. Pat Rush. With his permission, given in the summer of 1996, it is displayed here.

Albert Pickens retired from the Biological Survey in 1929 to his 320-acre ranch at Tres Piedras, NM. He built this small cabin and lived there until he moved to Hot Springs, NM about 1944. His ranch included part of the largest of the three rock formations from which Tres Piedras gets its name. The largest promontory is still known as Pickens Rock.

This was the first vehicle issued to Homer after his employment with the state. The passenger door is marked "State of New Mexico Game and Fish Dept. No. 8" and is probably a 1930 or 31 Ford panel truck pulling a trailer with Homer's horse, Skip.

Harry Shuart, editor of the *New Mexico Magazine,* made this photograph of Homer and his mule, Jeremiah, with three full grown lions when they hunted in Water and Frijoles Canyons in the Jemez Mountains in 1932. Mr. Shuart included the picture with his article in the October 1932 issue. This photo also appeared on the cover of the New Mexico brochure distributed at the Chicago World's Fair in 1933.

In 1934, Homer made this photo of an adult lion treed on a rocky ledge on Brushy Mountain in the Gila Wilderness. This large snarling lion has its rear feet as far back on its perch as can be imagined. Frank Hibben was with him on this hunt and later shot the lion. Pictured is Homer's hound, Booger, and nearest the lion is Chito, a mix of Airedale and German shepherd, much favored by Homer.

Pickens Bags Ten Mountain Lions In April; New Record

SANTA FE, May 4 (AP)—Elliott Barker, state game warden, said Saturday Hunter Homer Pickens of the state department broke his own record when he bagged ten mountain lions during the month of April in the Mogollon Mountains.

Barker said his best previous record for a month was nine and he had twice taken that number.

This article was published in *The Santa Fe New Mexican* in May 1932. News of Homer's exploits as a lion hunter from 1931 into the 1950s was published in newspapers and periodicals throughout New Mexico, Colorado and Texas.

In 1933 Homer caught this young mountain lion on Mogollón Creek and, with the help of Lawrence Shelley, roped and tied it. According to a newspaper article from Silver City, the half grown lion was promised to the city zoo in Clovis, New Mexico.

A. B. "Doc" Seitzler was well known throughout southwestern New Mexico for his bear hounds. Homer and Seitzler became friends when Homer hunted in the Gila and Black Range from 1928 to the 1940s. Doc Seitzler's artistry in making, not only beautiful, but rugged saddles brought him fame long after he passed away. He made one of his famous saddles for Homer in 1936.

Jack Pickens, left, with his older brother, Homer Jr., are pictured in Silver City, New Mexico in 1935. Jimmy was still a baby and Homer and Edna and their 3 boys lived temporarily in the home of Judge George Hay on 6th Street until Homer's promotion to district deputy game warden and transfer to Albuquerque the next year.

Highland Road in 1936 was not much more than a dirt trail north of Albuquerque. Homer rented this adobe house while it was still unfinished. Here he used the basement to hold his live beavers, Edna and Homer Jr. looked into the night sky for alien invaders and the boys rode their burro, Senorita. The three boys are lined up on their stick horses looking toward the Sandias ready to hit the trail.

Edna Pickens with her three boys, l to r, Jimmy, Jack and Homer Jr. at Panchuela Creek in the Pecos Wilderness. Jack and Homer Jr. wear fur coats made by Edna in 1937. By then, all the boys were fishermen and trout were plentiful in the Panchuela.

The Pickens boys, l to r, Homer Jr., Jack and Jimmy on the opening day of the 1938 fishing season. Jimmy is holding a large Rainbow trout caught about one mile below El Vado dam on the Chama River.

The three Pickens boys on Highland Road in Albuquerque with a wild burro they named "Senorita." At that time there were herds of wild burros on the Jemez National Forest. In 1938, Homer purchased a permit and caught this one for his sons. Homer Jr. was 7, Jack, 5 and Jimmy, 3.

Right, Jack Pickens holds a 20-inch Rainbow trout caught at Bluewater Lake about 1938. As the three boys were watching their bobbers and catching yellow perch a friend standing beside them landed this large Rainbow in an unusual catch. The next morning Homer caught an 18-inch German Brown on a dry fly in one of the small streams that feeds the lake.

Below, Homer with another of his best lion dogs, Buck. This picture was made within a year or two after the start of World War II. Homer sits on the running board of his patrol car, probably a 1940 Chevrolet, that lasted him until he was issued a war surplus jeep after the end of the war.

Homer with Yankee Dan, a descendant of one of the Slash Ranch Hounds. Yankee Dan was the pick of the litter of 12 puppies born in 1936 to Sue, one of Homer's best hounds. Yankee Dan died of coyote poison in 1938 while hunting lions in the Sandia Mountains.

Homer pictured in 1938 when he was 35 years old and had been in New Mexico for 11 years. He had set many records both in enforcing the state's game laws and in hunting mountain lions. By this time he had been a district deputy game warden for two years. Elliott Barker wrote, "He is without a doubt, one of the very best all around game men I have ever known."

Homer Jr. recalls fishing the Rio San Antonio on the Baca Ranch as early as 1939 at the age of 8. He fished intermittently through the Vietnam War years and later with his son and father until 1990. Homer made this photograph about 1941.

Left, Homer's middle son, Jack, helps his father release young ring neck pheasants in the Rio Grande valley south of Albuquerque about 1945. When the boys were old enough and school permitted, Homer had his sons with him as much as possible. The three lucky Pickens boys learned to love the outdoors and practice the fundamentals of wildlife conservation.

Below, Edna Pickens was a voracious and perceptive reader and the attack of December 7th, 1941 was of little surprise to her. That Christmas her boys were delighted with their gifts of toy helmets at their Pueblo Solano home. Playing soldier immediately became popular with the neighborhood children but by the time the war was over Homer Jr. was approaching the age to enter military service.

In the summer of 1944, Homer took members of Boy Scout Troop 29 from Santa Fe to the Jemez Mountains where they fished the Rio Cebolla. They left Santa Fe from the DeBolt residence on Palace Avenue and camped at the Fenton Rock House on the Cebolla where Fenton Lake now stands. Pictured from left to right are Homer Pickens, Jack Pickens (top of head), an unidentified boy, Bob Berntsen, Norman Brown, Dan Peterson, Homer Jr. and standing are Jimmy Pickens and Mr. Peterson. The three boys seated on the right side of the truck are Richard Bradford (wearing a cap and face concealed), Bob DeBolt (wearing hat and facing camera) and Louis Rockett with left arm on the tailgate.

Boy Scouts from Troop 29 in Santa Fe, l to r, in front, Richard Bradford in the sailor hat and Jack Pickens, standing behind are Dan Peterson and Homer Jr. This photo was made in the summer of 1944 on the outing at Seven Springs Fish Hatchery.

About 1899, Elijah McLean Fenton built a ten-room rock house on the hillside overlooking the Rio Cebolla. Pictured are Elijah McLean "Mac" Fenton, Jr. and his sister Jean Fenton in front of the landmark Fenton Rock House about 1903. Their father and mother Elijah Sr. and Jessie Lime Fenton are seated on the front porch. Homer and Albert were friends of the Fentons as early as they hunted and trapped through the Jemez country in the late 1920s. This landmark rock house was demolished by the State Parks Division in the mid 1980s. Use of this picture and information is by the courtesy of Mary Fenton Caldwell who owns the photograph.

The Pickens home shown in deep snow of the winter of 1946 when Betsy was one and a half years old. Jimmy is on the left and Jack on the right. In the coming spring the ground, then covered in snow, would be covered with giant red poppies. The old road to Pacheco Canyon and Chupadero passed in front of their Tesuque home.

Homer with his three boys, l to r, Jimmy, Jack and Homer Jr. Good friend, Harold Walter, made this photograph for Homer about 1947 in the Rio Grande Canyon near Embudo, New Mexico. Homer never missed an opportunity to take his sons with him in his travels.

Homer loved his four children, as Edna said, even more than his dogs and his horse. He also loved the outdoors and engendered the same love in his three sons and daughter. When she was eight years old, Homer carried Betty Ann across the Rio Grande to a choice fishing hole. Harold Walter made this photo about 1953 near Pilar, New Mexico.

The youngest Pickens child, Betsy, in 1951 holds a mountain lion kitten, one of the many young animals that lived temporarily at the Pickens' Tesuque home. Betsy was six at the time and the old Dockweiler ranch was much as it had been for many years.

Jimmy Pickens with a four-point buck he killed at a special hunt on the Philmont Boy Scout Ranch in the fall of 1951. Jimmy was 16 when he shot this buck in Ponil Canyon near the boundaries of the CS and Vermejo Park Ranches. Jimmy loved to hunt and like his two brothers also loved to fish.

When this picture was made in the den of their Tesuque home, the three Pickens boys were enrolled at New Mexico A & M College, now NM State University, and military service was not far away. Homer, Edna and Betsy were quite alone but with Homer's appointment as director of the department social responsibilities increased for them all. This photograph was made for an article which appeared in the May 1955 issue of *New Mexico Law,* a journal published by the New Mexico Sheriff and Police Association.

The official photograph of Homer C. Pickens, Director of the New Mexico State Department of Game and Fish. Homer commenced employment with the state in 1931 as a trapper and lion hunter and rose to become director in 1953, retiring in 1958.

Three retired directors and the sitting director of the New Mexico State Department of Game and Fish enjoy a social gathering in April 1978 at the Four Hills Country Club in Albuquerque. From l to r, are Director Harold Olsen and retired directors Bill Huey, Ladd Gordon and Homer Pickens.

Homer at the main gate of the Baca Ranch entering the Valle Caldera in deep winter snow. Homer worked for Pat Dunigan from 1971 to 1978 and continued to advise Mr. Dunigan on wildlife conservation matters for several years.

The Baca Ranch had a large population of coyotes and Homer used all his skill as a hunter and trapper to control them on the 100,000-acre cattle and wildlife operation. This very large coyote fell to Homer's skill with a predator call and his rifle. Homer was 75 years old at the time this photo was made.

With an armload of coyote pelts, Homer walks out of heavy snow in the fall of 1977 toward the front door of the "Movie House" at the Baca Ranch. Homer had been employed by Pat Dunigan for several years controlling the predators with his skill as a trapper. This photo was made for an *Albuquerque Journal* article which was published in the December 11, 1977 issue.

Homer with his grandson, Homer Christopher Pickens, III on the Rio San Antonio at the Baca Ranch in 1970. Homer taught Chris, age 6, to fly fish then they camped out on the ranch near the Rito de los Indios.

The U.S. Forest Service Smokey Bear stands with Homer Christopher Pickens, III at his grandfather's 90th birthday celebration. At the time, Homer's grandson, Chris, was a graduate student at Georgetown University.

Homer and Edna had eight grandchildren, now all adults with their own families. In their backyard at Los Alamos in 1965, Homer showed "Butch," Cynthia and Jennifer, as small children, how to feed a mule deer fawn. These three are the children of Homer and Edna's middle son, Jack and his wife Deanna (Donohoe) Pickens. Homer Jr. and his wife, Jo (Benson) have Chris; Jimmy and wife, Joana (Holterman), have two daughters, Kathy and Danette. Betsy and Max Cabber, Jr. have Tres and Michael.

Toward the end of his life, reminiscences of good friends were one of Homer's greatest rewards. Shown at Vermejo Park Ranch (above) on an elk hunt in 1949 were four of the best: Bert Clancy, United States Attorney; Tommy Holder, District Deputy Game Warden; Colin Neblett, United States Federal District Judge; and, Oscar Hawkins, Special Agent in Charge of the Santa Fe Field Office of the FBI. Through the years Smokey Bear (below) was a part of Homer's life. On his arrival in Santa Fe, in this rare photo, Smokey stood on the engine cowling of the Game Department's Piper Cub. Homer began Smokey's last airplane ride on June 27, 1950.

A game warden's kids (above) wearing tattered sweaters and with holes in their shoes have lunch on a rocky hillside in the Sandias in 1937. Their beagle "Primo" shared everything from their bedrolls to their canteen and sandwiches. These lucky boys loved the life made for them by their Mom and Dad. Forty three years later (below) the same boys with their little sister, Betsy, shared the joy of their Mother and Father's 50th wedding anniversary at Kirtland Air Force Base Officers Club in Albuquerque in 1980. L to r are Jack, Jimmy (Lt. Colonel, US Air Force), Edna, Homer, Betsy and Homer Jr. (Colonel, US Army).

Homer is greeted at his 90th birthday celebration by the quiet and friendly 7 foot Smokey Bear. This Smokey is a living, breathing icon always accompanied by an official representative. Pictured is Homer's good friend Bill Chapel, Assistant Director of Fire Management for the Forest Service's Southwestern Region. The *Albuquerque Journal* covered the event with a front-page photo and article on July 5, 1993.

The Smokey Bear hot air balloon operated by the U.S. Forest Service traveled throughout the United States. In 1993 the Smokey balloon came to Augusta, GA and Homer Jr. visited Bill Chapel and the famous balloon his father had helped create. The *Augusta Chronicle* covered the event with an article and photos on October 17, 1993.

CHAPTER 1

A NEW LIFE IN NEW MEXICO

IT WAS IN 1927. I was twenty-three, I had five dollars in my pocket and I was on my way to a new job in a strange land. At last, I was about to set foot in Albuquerque, New Mexico. I had already missed it once. The conductor had awakened me to inform me that we were on our way to Arizona and suggested that I might wish to debark in the little Indian village of Laguna, some seventy-eight miles (by rail) *beyond* Albuquerque. I had to catch the next train back to Albuquerque!

My world to this point had been limited to the flatlands and low rolling hills of Texas and Oklahoma. I knew little of any land beyond, especially New Mexico, but it mattered little, for as I would soon learn, no one could have prepared me for what I would find. Had I tried intentionally, I could not have found a more unusual state in which to begin a new life.

I had come to New Mexico at the suggestion of my half brother, Albert Pickens, who by this time had become a well known trapper for the U. S. Biological Survey (which a few years later, in about 1935, would become the U. S. Fish and Wildlife Service). Albert had written to me in Borger, Texas, where I was working in the oil fields for Phillips Petroleum Company. With the hope that I might be interested in joining him, he had enclosed instructions telling me who to contact so I could find his camp. I had decided to accept his invitation.

As I stepped off the train in Albuquerque on the first part of my journey, I was unaware that those few steps were to be the beginning of a lifelong trek during which I would cover thousands upon thousands of miles across almost every part of the state. In my travels I would find joy, friendship, adventure and personal fulfillment. Fortunately, I was unaware that I would also find anguish and disillusionment.

It was the first day of May, and it was glorious. The sky was vivid blue, and the air was pleasantly warm and refreshing. As I got out of the train and looked up, I was amazed by the magnificent building standing before me. I had never seen anything quite like it. It was the Alvarado Hotel. The architecture was that of a Spanish mission with deep porticos, long arched corridors and stately towers. I later found out it was built in 1905 by Fred Harvey and was commonly called the Station Hotel. However, it was named after Hernando de Alvarado, a captain of Coronado's famous expedition of 1540-1543 through what is now Mexico and the Southwestern United States. Captain Alvarado was the discoverer of the Buffalo (Great) Plains and the Indian pueblos of Acoma, Tiguex, Taos and Pecos.

In 1927, this hotel bearing Alvarado's name was a busy place—and with good reason. It was right next door to the train station, and passenger trains were then the quickest and easiest method of crossing the country. Albuquerque was an important stop on the line. The town was the center of activity in the state, and all the activity began, or ended, at the Alvarado. Albuquerque was proud of the hotel. It was a show place.

From the brick walk next to the train, I descended the few steps and walked into the hotel, winding my way through the bustling crowd. The dining rooms were packed. I was fascinated with the decor showing Spanish and Indian influence, and with the massive furniture. I wanted to see more, but I decided not to tarry. I found the First Street exit and stepped out into the big city. Almost all of the buildings on the west side of First Street were built closely together, forming a solid wall that towered above me. My route was straight ahead. I came to Gold Avenue, stopped and looked one block northward, where I could see the sparks flying above the electric streetcars and hear the humming sound that the cars made as they moved east and west along Central Avenue. As in the Alvarado, there

A NEW LIFE IN NEW MEXICO

were people everywhere. For a young man from a small town, the sights and sounds were awesome.

My instructions from Albert led me four blocks west on Gold Avenue, where I found the offices of the U.S. Biological Survey in the red stone French Building. On the lot where it was now stands the glass tower of the Sandia Savings Building. Across the street from the French Building were the Federal Building and the gold domed Post Office Building, both of which are still used for U. S. Government offices.

None of the people in the Biological Survey offices knew I was coming or knew anything about me, but when I introduced myself as the brother of Albert Pickens; I was immediately welcomed by all, including John Gatlin, who was rodent control supervisor, and A. E. Gray, who was the New Mexico State supervisor for the survey. Rooms were available upstairs for visiting employees of the survey, and one was graciously offered to me for the night. With my limited funds, I, of course, accepted the offer. John Gatlin began immediately to make arrangements for me to ride on the following day with the postman who would be northbound for Cuba, my next stop towards Albert's camp.

Early the next morning I met the postman and boarded a Model T Ford. It was another beautiful day. There were a few people on the streets—some waiting for the streetcars. I saw men wearing straw hats and dressed in blue jeans—called Levi jeans in those days—the first I had ever seen. I noticed that some of the Indians wore large black cowboy hats and had their shirttails out. These were the Navajos. Other Indians had blankets wrapped around their bodies. I learned that they were from pueblos near Albuquerque. The ranchers were easy to spot—they all wore cowboy boots.

At this time, the population of Albuquerque was about 27,000. Nearly all of the town was in the Rio Grande valley bottom or close to it. As we traveled northward on Fourth Street, the concrete pavement ended abruptly, and we entered the farmlands and the orchards. Water seemed to be everywhere, and cattails grew up next to the road, almost blocking our view of the fields beyond. Our path was about the only thing that resembled a road, and I silently wondered if it would continue beyond each next sand hill. Those little sand hills were the plague of all automobiles. The road went through one sand hill after another, and sooner or later one or more of them would trap almost every car. When we reached Los Ranchos de Albuquerque and the Alameda Church, I could see a thick forest, or bosque as it is called, westward toward the Rio Grande We passed through numerous small alfalfa fields until we reached Bernalillo, a small town which consisted of two or three blocks of buildings along one amazingly dirty street. The bridge westward over the Rio Grande was made of wood and was quite shaky. I was relieved to be across until I spotted more sand hills, larger and even more menacing than the ones we had already passed. I developed an admiration for the postman. He had obviously driven the road many times, and although there was not a single bridge from the Rio Grande to San Isidro, we tore through the sand without incident. San Isidro then was perhaps slightly smaller than it is today. There were two filling stations, two stores, a church, a bar and a few houses. Some of the men worked for the New Mexico Lumber Company sawmill at Gillman.

North of San Isidro, the road was not much more than a wagon trail. When we had traveled about one and a half miles, I spotted something new—"mud pots" as they were called. The mud pots were small mounds about four feet across, with thick mud continually bubbling upwards from a hole in the center. During the winter, steam could be seen rising from the mud, and it had a strong odor of sulphur. Years later, I would learn from a geologist friend that the area of the mud pots and northward, a very large fault in the rocks below the surface had caused the earth to shift and had formed the Nacimiento Mountains. Great pressures from within the earth had forced one side of the break upward to form the mountains. In the area of the mud pots and along the fault zone, ground water is warmed by the high temperatures of the deep rocks. Sulphur is picked up and carried to the surface as the water seeks to escape along the fault zone. North about five miles from the mud pots, we passed a hot spring probably also related to the faulting that uplifted the Nacimiento Mountains. Later, I would camp by the mud pots because there was abundant grass for the horses and a spring for water. The water for drinking was fair, if one did not mind the sulphur smell. A few years after we passed through, a well was drilled near the spring, and a small hotel was built to accommodate visitors who believed the water to be therapeutic.

The countryside was fascinating. Never before had I seen such a variety of colors. We had come through the many shades of green in the Rio Grande Valley, with the craggy imposing gray granite peaks of the Sandia Mountains reaching to over ten thousand feet above sea level a few miles to the east, through the smooth and graceful slopes of the tan sand hills and the nearby flat-topped mesas capped by black lava flows from ancient volcanoes, to the brilliant red of the rocks and soil north of San Isidro.

As we neared La Ventana, a little coal mining town, which in English means "the window" so called because there is a gap in the hills where the Rio Puerco ("dirty river") has cut through on its southward course, I became aware that with each mile we were climbing and the vegetation was changing. I began to see ponderosa pine trees sprinkling the higher areas nearby. La Ventana in those days was an active small coal mining town. The Santa Fe and Northwestern Railroad had been constructed from Bernalillo to the little town. Originally, it had been intended that the railroad would be built to Cuba, but financial problems and the added cost of construction through the more harsh terrain north of La Ventana had prevented it. There was a country store and one filling station (as they were called then). Gasoline for automobiles was pumped from a fifty-gallon steel drum. There was a hotel, at least that was what it was called. It did not resemble any hotel I had ever seen, but as I recollect, very few things I saw in New Mexico in 1927 resembled anything I had ever seen. There were about fifty inhabitants in the village. Most of the men worked in the mines, but the store, and especially the bar, also attracted many sheepherders, miners, and cowboys, from the nearby ranches.

As we approached Cuba, the pine trees were more abundant.

We were in the high country well above 6,000 feet. There seemed to be something new around each curve in the road. Had it been necessary to turn back at that point, the trip would already have been worthwhile.

Cuba, formerly named Nacimiento ("Nativity"), had four stores, two filling stations, a post office and the John Young Hotel. Primarily, the economy was based on sheep herding. Nearby was a sawmill, and east of town in Señorita Canyon was a copper mine. The population was probably not more than 700. I observed that nearly all of the people were either of Spanish descent or were Navaho Indians. Since my first observations when I stepped off the train in Albuquerque, I had continued to marvel at the contrasts. Not only was the landscape always changing, but each town was different, and now the people were different. Would any two places be alike? I hoped not—and I was not to be disappointed in the years to come.

I spent the night in the John Young Hotel. The main room of the hotel was known far and wide—and small wonder. In it was a round sunken fireplace that could accommodate logs five feet long. John Young and his wife were gracious hosts, and the memories I have of them and of the cozy hours I spent that night in front of that fireplace are among my fondest.

The following morning the postman and I left the Model T in Cuba and continued northward to Lindrith in a wagon. It would be several years before the roads in this area were ready for automobiles. I spent the night in Lindrith with Mr. and Mrs. Hill, who ran the post office and country store. The next morning two young girls, the Bishop sisters, arrived. Fortunately, when they learned that I was Albert's brother, they offered to take me to his camp. The girls doubled up on one of their horses, and I rode the other to their home. Their father was a farmer, and the family lived near Tapacitos, a post office and store about four miles north of Lindrith. From their farm, one of the girls continued with me to Albert's camp.

Albert was somewhat surprised when I rode into camp, especially since I was riding a fine black horse! I assured him that I was not that affluent. Almost without further thought, he decided that the very first order of business must be that I have a horse, so we rode back to the Bishops' to ask if they would sell the one I had ridden to his camp. A short while later he purchased the animal and saddle at a bargain for a hundred dollars.

With the most important task disposed of (without a horse I could not help on the trap line or help move the camp), Albert, assuming correctly that I had come to work, immediately began my training. Meanwhile, he wrote to the Albuquerque office to ask if I could be employed, and his superiors agreed to hire me as "camp helper," at one dollar per day plus chuck. My gear had to come by mail. In the meantime, I had to bunk with Albert. His bedroll was light, and I remember particularly on May 8, 1927, Mother's Day, I was very glad to be sharing his bedroll, because I woke startled to find it had snowed about eight inches of heavy wet snow while we slept.

Albert was a gentle and pleasant man, and to my good fortune he was also very patient. He loved his work with the U. S. Biological Survey, and was always happy and smiling. His customary dress was Levi jeans and jacket, leather chaps, and cowboy boots with small spurs. He had a black saddle horse which was larger than the one he had purchased for me. His horse did not like spurs, large or small. That animal would tolerate spurs only to a certain point, and when he could finally take them no longer, he bucked and often unceremoniously dumped Albert. Some days something in his character gave him the urge, and he just had to buck.

My fun began when Albert started teaching me camp duties. My first job was to feed the animals. He had three pack animals and two saddle horses, and of course there was my little black horse. I had to care for all of them. When it came to camp cooking, which is an art itself, or washing dishes, I was a genuine greenhorn. I had never seen a dutch oven or the special copper bean pot which we buried in the ground beside glowing wood coals to cook the beans (or "frijoles" as I learned beans were called in New Mexico). Albert had two dutch ovens, one for meat and one for biscuits. A dutch oven has legs and is set over an open fire. It has a heavy iron lid and a rim to hold coals. The coals below and atop the oven are to maintain an even temperature for whatever is cooked. The biscuits were delicious whenever Albert cooked them. When I was cooking and the wind blew I burned everything—bread, meat or even the beans, if they were over the fire and not still in the ground. Albert always kept a neat and clean camp. He insisted that the dishes be scalded after they were washed, and it was done no matter whether it was raining or snowing. He was a meticulous man, but in his business a man had to be or he was not successful.

Albert had two well-trained hound dogs named Sam and Nig, which he used for hunting mountain lions. Sam would sit beside Albert and never touch a thing while we were eating. Then, when we were finished Albert would prepare the dogs' food in separate pans. He also had a young hound named Beaver. Beaver was always into something, a genuinely mischievous pup. It seemed to me that he gave Albert a lot of trouble, but, as I discovered in raising my own hounds in the following years, he was just typical.

Slowly I learned. From cooking, I progressed to the art of placing a pack saddle on a pack horse, and this was no easy task. The horses would not stand still until I could get the belly band fastened and had all the snaps and buckles fastened on the britching (the harness that keeps the pack saddle solidly on the horse). Next I learned to pack the heavy canvas panniers, each equal in weight to keep from hurting the horses' backs, and to hang one on each side of the pack saddle. Having mastered this, I progressed to covering the entire pack with a canvas cover. The last step was to tie the pack rope, which was about twenty feet long, around the animal and pack several different ways so that a diamond hitch knot could be tied on top. This arrangement kept the pack on the horse up and down hills and was very important, because even if the horse bucked, the pack would stay on.

When I graduated from the course on camp procedures and packing, Albert began to take me with him to check his trap lines, and I started my first lessons in handling trapping equipment. At last the time for the major event had arrived. Trapping lobos was Albert's speciality, and he was an artist. His dogs, Sam and Nig, were trained only for lions and bobcats. They would not, for example, chase a bear. If some of the traps were set with drag hooks, whatever was caught in the trap would drag the trap away, and sometimes Albert would use the dogs to locate the animal and the trap. We were always careful to visit each trap every other day—or sooner. There were two reasons for this: one was to insure that no animal had to stay in the trap very long, and the other was to check the traps to see if any livestock had thrown them, which frequently happened. If the traps were thrown, we had to reset or relocate them, depending upon the circumstances.

Within a short time, Mr. A. E. Gray, who was the U. S. Biological Survey's New Mexico district manager for predatory animal and rodent control, came to our camp for a visit. By this time we had moved from Tapacitos to French Mesa near the Gallina post office. On the way to Gallina we had passed the Costilla post office. It seemed as if there were post offices behind almost every tree in those days. Most of the post offices are gone now, but in those days the public land in that area was open for homesteading and had been since shortly after World War I. Many war veterans and others had homesteaded throughout a widely scattered area from Chama to Taos, making the many small post offices necessary. The Tierra Amarilla Land Grant, of course, was not included for homesteading, but several people bought small tracts from the people of Spanish descent who still owned the land. There were also many little country stores that literally sold anything made. On my first trip to one of these stores, I quickly joined the Levi Strauss gang, complete with full jeans attire—jacket, shirt, pants, and, of course, boots.

From the post office and store at Gallina, we roamed to other post offices at Capulin, Coyote and Cañones, near where the Abiquiu Dam now stands across the Chama River. My tracks were already stretching across scores of miles. By mid-summer we arrived on the Tusas River in the Brazos meadow country north of Tierra Amarilla, where the summer range was dotted with thousands of sheep. The magnificence of this country was another delightful contrast for me. Precipitation is greater in this area than in the country we had left, and the vegetation is more abundant and variable. We traveled over the main divide above the present Hopewell Lake and into Tres Piedras. I met many of the ranchers in the area who were to become my life-long friends. On the Tusas, I met Oscar Royal and his family. Oscar was having problems with lobo wolves, which were killing whiteface cows and young cattle that were grazing in the high country. Later, in the fall, Oscar helped us in our efforts to trap the wolves. Albert and I spent the remainder of the summer traveling to Taos and Chama and into Colorado, all the while checking carefully for wolf signs and discussing the problem with the ranchers. Wolves also included sheep in their diet, and the sheep ranchers were suffering financially.

By early fall we began in earnest to trap the wolves. We had located their range and were ready to do what we could to stop the livestock destruction. At first we set only a few traps, but we soon found that the country was so overrun with coyotes that they were the only thing we could catch. We concentrated our efforts in the high country at the head of the Brazos River and down the divide to the Canjilon Creek and to El Rito, but still the only thing we caught were coyotes. We averaged about one coyote each day for six weeks. We observed that the porcupine population was extremely high, and they were heavily damaging both young and old pine trees by chewing off the bark in a ring around the tree, causing the tree to die. As winter set in and the snow deepened, I noted with interest that the porcupines were similar to human tourists traveling across country and spending the night in hotels. The porcupines would travel perhaps 100 yards in the deep snow using only one path from one tree to another and would then stay in the tree for a day or two before moving on. A few days later I would notice other porcupines in the same tree. Nearby trees would be avoided and those certain "hotel" trees always chosen. Albert reported the abundance of the porcupines to the Forest Service, and we were asked to reduce their population, which we did to a certain extent.

Finally, after also reducing the coyote population in the

area where we knew the wolves were roaming, we succeeded in trapping seven lobos. So far as I know, these were the last wolves to roam that country. No rancher has ever reported losing any more cattle to wolves. Although I fully understood the situation both then and now, to this day I regret that it had to be. Oscar Royal, were he alive today, and all the other ranchers who were fighting for survival (and the destruction by the wolves did make it difficult to survive) would all agree that though it had to be, still, the wolves were beautiful, majestic animals. We heard them howl a few times, not often, because they were shy. Their howl was coarse and deep, quite unlike the shrill yip of the coyote. Whenever I heard them, the sound always brought to me an awareness of the vastness and loneliness of that country, a feeling that I imagine was apparent to newcomers and old-timers alike.

Later, in 1933 or 1934, John Davenport, who at one time was part owner of the Baca Location No. 1, a huge tract of land in the Jemez Mountains, killed a lobo wolf between Ojo Caliente and Tres Piedras. John and his partners ran sheep in the valley between Taos and Tres Piedras. Early one morning John spotted a wolf at close range in the sagebrush. He shot it with his Colt six gun and subsequently had the animal mounted. His wife, Frances, later gave the mounted wolf to me to donate to the Los Alamos museum, which is housed in the building that formerly was the main lodge for the old Los Alamos Ranch School.

After Albert and I trapped the seven wolves, we checked the area along the Colorado line west from the Rio Grande to the Four Corners area for additional wolf signs but found no more. Doubling back, we made camp near the old stockyards in both Chama and Tres Piedras. At Tres Piedras we rode the narrow gauge, known as the "Chili Line" to Española and Santa Fé for supplies. Riding that little train was quite a thrill.

Santa Fé was the most unusual town I had yet seen. Smaller than Albuquerque, it was the second largest town in New Mexico. I don't know what I expected of the capital of this state, but by then I should have been prepared. I wasn't. It was, and still is, a quaint city. Probably the most striking sights for me were the flat buildings and the smoke. Spires of smoke gave the appearance of a ghostly forest rising above the single level dwellings. Everywhere I looked in the streets I saw burros packing unbelievable loads of the cherished aromatic piñon wood. It was a thriving business. It had to be to keep all of those fireplaces burning! At the time we were in Santa Fé nearly all of the buildings I saw were made of adobe. Although I did see a few made of brick. There were plenty of covered wagons which were not unusual in those days. The population was an interesting blend. There was about an equal number of Spanish, Indians and Anglos—a word generally accepted in New Mexico to represent collectively, all the ethnic types other than Spanish and Indian. In all, I found it to be a captivating place, and, although we did not tarry long, I hoped that I would have the opportunity to see more of it someday. The beginning of a wide spectrum of memories connected with Santa Fé was still to be a few years away, however, and as we caught the little train back to our camp I was unaware of the important role this city would play in my life.

From Tres Piedras we moved to the Valle Grande ("Great Valley"), a breathtaking place in the Jemez Mountains which in my opinion is probably the most beautiful mountain valley in all of the southwest. The Valle is part of a volcanic complex the result of a collapse of the earth's crust after volcanic eruptions spewed out many cubic miles of debris. The Valle and surrounding mountains have been privately owned throughout this century and with the exclusion of timber cutting, remain mostly unchanged from the same pristine condition as when I first gazed upon the area in 1927. The Valle bottom is practically treeless. For thousands of years after the volcanoes died, the Valle could not drain, and a huge lake covered the Valle floor. Erosion finally cut through the rim of the valley and outward drainage was established by the perennial streams, the San Antonio Creek and the Jemez River. The Valle Grande meadow, formerly covered by the lake is about twelve miles across and is now covered with grass in the summer and abundant snow in the winter. Redondo, the highest peak in the mountains surrounding the Valle, rises majestically on the west side of the valley to 11,254 feet above sea level and along with the other peaks is covered with scrub oak, blue spruce, aspen and ponderosa pine. The Valle Grande and the Jemez Mountains have played a memorable role in my life, and still do.

While we were in the Valle Grande on that first visit together, Albert and I checked for wolf signs and found none. We did, however, manage to get a few mountain lions near the old Pine Springs Ranger Station, which was just north of the Los Alamos Ranch School. The lions were wreaking havoc on horses kept in the area. We managed to thin out the lions, and the problem was eliminated.

From this area we moved to the abandoned mining town of Bland, southwest of the Valle Grande. It was an intriguing little place nestled in a steep narrow canyon so small that I wondered how there was room for all the activity that I imagined must have taken place in its heyday. I would like to have been there to witness the mining, milling and excitement generated by the possibility of untold fortunes. But that all had occurred before I was born, and, as I later learned, the fortunes, considering the cost and time involved, were not great. Bland was a part of the Cochiti mining district, which also encompassed other areas outside of this canyon. The district between 1893 and 1904 produced gold and silver valued at $1,321,582. Various problems, especially the lack of water, gradually forced operations to shut down, and although attempts have been made to revive the mining, none has succeeded. In 1927, when we were there, the only inhabitants were Mr. Lemley, the forest ranger, and his wife.

A. E. Gray, the state supervisor for the survey joined us in Bland and brought some news that left me with mixed emotions. The office in Albuquerque had decided my initial training period was over and that it was time for me to move on. It had been so pleasant working with Albert that I felt somewhat reluctant to leave, although I concealed my thoughts, for I was grateful that the Survey was apparently satisfied with my work and I was anxious to progress and to earn my pay, which incidentally had already been increased to seventy dollars per month. I had been with Albert about thirteen months, and I was thoroughly convinced that this was my way of life. As Mr. Gray and I left Bland in a government car, I thought about the past year and about how fortunate I had been to spend that time with a brother I had never really known before. Oh, he had come home to visit a few times when I was younger, but I had always been somewhat awed by this relative stranger who led such a fascinating life. Now I had gotten this chance to know him well and to share his way of life. My thoughts turned then to the other members of my family and to my early days in Texas and Oklahoma.

CHAPTER 2

MY EARLY DAYS

MY GRANDFATHER, William Pickens, was born on March 5, 1824, in McNairy County, Tennessee. On October 29, 1848, he married Mary Jennettie Robertson in Hardin County, Tennessee, and their first child, William Matthew, my father, was born on February 22, 1851. Two more children were born before the family migrated to Arkansas. At the time of the move, my father was about five years old. After a short stay in Arkansas, the family moved again when grandfather heard about some farm land that was available for homesteading a short distance west around the small community of Blackjack, Texas, near Sulphur Springs, the seat of Hopkins County, Texas. In their new home, six more children were born. During the Civil War, grandfather was in the Confederate Army and served as a captain. Following the war, he resumed his primary trade, which was the making of furniture. The income from his trade was supplemented by farming. At least one piece, a table that he made in 1876, still survives intact.

My father did not follow my grandfather in the furniture business. He turned instead to farming for his livelihood. On August 1, 1882, he married Celia Jane Brumlow, and they settled in Hunt County, Texas. Two sons were born: William Lonzo, or Lonnie, as he was called throughout his life, on March 16, 1884, and Joseph Albert on November 6, 1885. Albert was to become probably the single most important influence on my life and career. Death took Celia Jane early and a few years later, after moving back to Hopkins County, my father married Belle Jones, my mother, on November 26, 1899.

My father had a medium build. He kept his hair trimmed neatly and was always clean-shaven, except for a mustache. A pleasant and congenial man, he was constantly ready to help his neighbors. He loved singing conventions and church meetings. Above all, he loved his fellow man and instilled honesty in his children, always insisting that they must pay their debts and keep their word. He enjoyed good health throughout most of his life, which lasted eighty-two years.

My mother was an attractive, trim woman who had been reared on a farm and was well acquainted with all the chores required, both inside and outside of the house. My father and mother belonged to the Baptist-Presbyterian church. Mother was a very kindly and friendly person who cherished her neighbors. Just as her own parents had trained her, she made sure that each of the children, especially the girls, were also well trained in the family chores. Never given to panic, she could handle any emergency that arose. As an example, our house was next to the railroad, and on one occasion a passing train showered the roof of the house with cinders, igniting the shingles. Mother immediately took charge and formed a bucket brigade with the children. With her guidance, we successfully extinguished the fire even though we had to climb the ladder repeatedly to do so. The railroad repaired the damage to the house within a few days.

William Ernest was born on September 18, 1900. I was born July 5, 1903, and was followed by Roy on September 26, 1906, Essie Fay on September 20, 1909, and Reba on December 19, 1915. Ernest died in 1949 from meningitis following a fall in an accident in a cotton seed oil mill where he worked. He is buried in Durant, Oklahoma, in the cemetery near my mother. His two sons were career military men and are now retired. Roy married twice, had one adopted daughter, and passed away some years ago. Essie married David Earnest, and they have three children. Dave ran a nursery, and he and Essie are now living in retirement in Durant, Oklahoma. Reba's husband, Edward David Airington, a Choctaw Indian of Durant, worked for Phillips Petroleum Company. He died in Borger, Texas, of a heart attack. Reba also now lives in Durant, Oklahoma.

MY EARLY DAYS

Life on a farm in the early 1900's could be summed up in two words: Hard Work! There were few conveniences, and we had to build, grow, care for, harvest, preserve or store almost everything we had. The nearest store was four miles away in Cumby, Texas. Except for the occasional purchase of necessities such as seed or animals and certain articles of clothing, tools or foodstuffs, we seldom bought anything else, because money was scarce and hard to come by. The work varied with the season. In the spring, we plowed and planted. In the summertime, while the crops were growing, we cut oak and ricked it into cords to sell in town or to dry for the winter. We had a crosscut saw seven feet long on which we took turns and then stacked the wood in ricks, which were four by four by eight foot stacks. Two ricks made a cord. As crops matured, we had fresh vegetables on the table and began to store them for the winter. In the late fall we picked cotton and harvested corn and grain. Also in the fall, we generally butchered four or five fat hogs and a calf after the weather began to turn cool. Whenever butchering time came, the whole community would get together and all share in the work. When hogs were butchered and the meat was cut and cooled, the pork was salted and put into the smokehouse for curing. The only fresh pork we ate were the bony parts and the bacon sides, which were always too fatty. The good parts, the hams, were put away in preservatives, country style, and were not eaten until the next summer. The home curing process for hams left much to be desired. The hams were terribly salty. To this day I still cringe, whenever I recall the taste. I have to admit that even though it was a way to save meat until it was needed, it nevertheless always seemed to me to be a waste of good meat. It delights me that the salt curing process we used has become a thing of the past.

Another project that was time consuming but important to our livelihood was the making of ribbon cane syrup from sugar cane which we grew in the river bottom. We cut the cane and stripped off the leaves to obtain stalks about six to eight feet in length. I always loved the taste of the fresh juice when the stalks were run through the mill. The mill was built on a hill. It had three vertical rollers with a long pole for a lever.

A horse was hitched to a pole attached to a gear mechanism and walked continuously around the mill to provide the power for operating the mill. The cane stalks were pushed through the rollers to squeeze out the juice, which drained into a catch pan and then downhill into vats. The vats were about one foot deep, six feet wide and twenty feet long. Cord wood was used to fire the furnace below the vats. A thermometer was used to test the syrup. If the syrup was cooked too long it turned into sugar; if not cooked long enough, it fermented. The syrup was stored in one-gallon containers. Choice stalks were not run through the mill, but instead were planted in the creek bottom and, if they had a bud along the stem, would take root and grow. We also grew sorghum cane in the higher areas of our land and made syrup from it, but it was not nearly so sweet as the ribbon cane syrup.

Nearly all of the homes in the area were wooden, and ours was no exception. There were two big bedrooms, a kitchen with a large wood-burning stove, dining room, living room (or front room) with a fireplace, a long front porch across the full length of the house where we slept in the summer, and an L-shaped back porch. Outside were the outhouse, smokehouse and storm cellar. The smokehouse was ten by twelve feet and carefully boarded to make it airtight. The storm cellar was excavated six to eight feet below the ground surface and covered with logs, boards and dirt. We also called it the "scardey hole" because that was where we fled, generally in May, when we thought there might be a tornado in the vicinity. Anyone who has lived very long in tornado country watches the sky carefully when the clouds build and learns quickly to recognize the dangerous formations and head for the cellar. We stored canned vegetables and fruit on shelves built into the walls of the storm cellar. The even temperature enabled us to keep pumpkins, turnips, potatoes, sweet potatoes, carrots, beets and cabbages through midwinter.

I remember the fireplace especially well. One evening when I was about five, as I walked in front of the fireplace, I stubbed my toe on Ernest's feet, fell backward and sat down on the hot coals. I burned by buttock and carry the scar today. Mother, as usual, rose to the situation and treated the burn with a poultice. By necessity she treated most of our injuries with home remedies. We were fortunate that she had been well taught.

When I was about twelve years old, Dad bought a small blacksmith outfit and taught us to sharpen a plow. We were able to do a fair job, but when the plows were bent we had to take them to a specialist, the blacksmith, who could reshape them for us. The blacksmith, Mr. Robinson, had his shop in Brashear, a small community between Sulphur Springs and Cumby. He had ten children, all of whom are living today. One son, Jack, and I were the same age and were schoolmates. Jack is now a prominent businessman in Amarillo, Texas. One Saturday afternoon, when Jack and I were about eleven, Dad took Roy and me into Brashear to have Mr. Robinson do some work for us. When we arrived, I met Jack, and we wandered across the street to the barbershop. As we stepped up onto the boardwalk, a shot rang out. Dewey Stewart, a boy we knew, staggered through the door of the barbershop and fell dead on the boardwalk in front of us. We stood there horrified.

Dewey had been shot by Bill English, a neighbor of ours. This sad incident greatly impressed me. I was saddened for both boys. It was so needless. The two boys had been dating the same girl, and they had developed a grudge that culminated in the tragedy. English, who was about seventeen, thought that he was the regular boyfriend of the girl. He had arrived in his buggy at the rear entrance of the barbershop when he encountered Dewey. An argument erupted, and, as they started in the back door, Bill, who was carrying a .22 caliber pistol, shot Dewey, who then ran through the shop before he fell where we stood. Bill's father owned a large ranch and was rather prominent and influential and consequently was able to put the trial off until feelings diminished somewhat. When Bill finally was tried, he was given a suspended sentence. Later in life he owned the Red Ball bus line, which operated between Dallas, Fort Worth and Amarillo. He died of a heart attack.

One of my favorite pastimes on the farm was squirrel hunting. The hunting season was in the fall, and we never missed bringing home several fox squirrels, which were plentiful in the area. We considered them a delicacy. It seemed to me a bigger thrill to hunt squirrel than quail, because we could always trap quail in midwinter when the squirrels hibernated. Always, just before Christmas, after we had gathered the crops of corn and oats and had picked all the cotton, we would set our quail traps by the old well next to the briar patch and along the field fence where there was a lot of vegetation. In this area grew berry vines, persimmon trees and oak brush, all of which provided feed for the quail. We never trapped all the quail in a covey. Dad saw to that. We had to release some of them or make sure that the traps were moved before we caught the entire covey. That way we had quail year after year. We heard that some deer were hunted in southeast Texas in the deep woods, but in our area there were none.

Another of our favorite pastimes was our homespun version of a rodeo. Several of our neighbors, especially Floyd Mosley, one of my good friends to this day, would join us on a Saturday or Sunday afternoon to ride milk pen calves, some of which weighed four or five hundred pounds. One day when Mother and Dad had gone to town, leaving us at home, we decided it was time to practice. It fell my lot to try to ride the big one. I did not get far. It bucked me off into the manure pile, kicked me, and to make sure I got the message, stepped on me. Scar number two is on my left leg as a reminder.

On the infrequent Saturday we could get to Cumby, Dad would give each of us fifty cents to spend. We would spend ten cents for a picture show, five cents for a soft drink and five cents for all the candy we wanted. The money that was left we would spend on treating one another to whatever else we could buy. There were no fancy restaurants, but it didn't matter. When lunchtime arrived, although we usually were not hungry, we all had to meet at the country store where Dad would see that we had plenty of cheese and crackers and sometimes cookies and bananas. I recall that for some reason it always fascinated me to watch the clerk with his special cheese cutter slice off a chunk of cheese from the large round mold. The crackers were kept in a cracker barrel. When we ate our cheese and crackers we sat on a bench or a nail keg near the old potbellied stove. Some of the men who came into the store chewed tobacco and used as a spittoon a big bucket that sat next to the stove. I don't recall that it ever bothered my appetite particularly. After lunch we went to the movies. We had to be careful to get back to the wagon in time to return home by dark, because we had to feed and milk the cows, feed the hogs, chickens and the other livestock that we had.

After chores, it was usually time for bed, because we had to get up early. Occasionally we were permitted to stay up later. On one such evening, about the end of World War I, one of the neighbor boys began tinkering with a radio set. It was a small crystal set with earphones. At night he could receive a Dallas station that was about seventy-five to eighty miles west of us and was the only radio station in the area. We could barely stand the noise of the station as it surged in loudly, but we were even more irritated when it faded out and we lost it completely. This was my first experience with a radio.

We had a telephone, a square box thing that hung on the wall, too high for the kids to reach. We had to stand on a chair to talk to anyone. The telephone was battery operated, and we had to turn a crank to ring for our friends and neighbors. The most important use for it by the youngsters was to arrange a basketball game or to plan a fishing trip down at the creek.

Of course like all youngsters we had to flap our wings once in awhile. I remember Mrs. Robinson (no relation to the blacksmith) was the school teacher who taught the classes from the first through the seventh grades. Mr. Woods, who had to use crutches due to an attack of polio in his youth, taught the eighth through the twelfth grades. We had to walk three miles one way to school. On rainy days we moved a lot of mud back and forth between home and school when that goo stuck to our shoes. The school had outdoor toilets, of course, and at the end of the schoolhouse there was a cistern which was filled from pipes around the eaves of the building to catch rainwater for us to drink. One memorable day, two or three of my friends and I slipped away from school for a rendezvous with a can of Prince Albert tobacco that we had hidden earlier by a fence post. Unfortunately Mr. Woods caught us, and during a severe tongue lashing he decided to single me out as the one who had stashed the can of tobacco. I was awarded several licks from his belt. The incident did not lower my opinion of Mr. Woods, however. He was a fine man and a good teacher—and I never did learn to smoke.

We had a dirt basketball court. With the help of nearby farmers we scraped, leveled, and marked the ground and put up the basket with a backstop. The boys and girls each had a team. The fashionable feminine dress for basketball was a black blouse and large black bloomers fastened below the knees. The boys wore "overhauls." Because travel was slow in those days, it was too difficult for one school to play against another, so our only competitors were our classmates. The boys often played basketball against the girls—perfectly acceptable then, but not in these days.

For other entertainment we were allowed to attend square dances, provided there were plenty of adult chaperones present. We were not allowed to play cards or even own a deck of cards —the result of the Baptist, Methodist and Presbyterian code. The first deck of cards I ever saw belonged to one of the neighbor boys, who had bought the cards in Sulphur Springs. We would meet him on Sunday afternoons under the bridge at the creek and would watch him, hoping to learn to play poker. We learned very little. I suspect that our teacher was not too adept, and, naturally, we had no way to practice, so the strict rules imposed on us concerning cards were most effective in spite of our indiscretions.

We attended church regularly, traveling in our wagon or in a neighbor's wagon. The church was a community church, Presbyterian and Methodist. Whenever revival meetings were held, we would attend every day. In the summer when the weather was damp and hot, everyone would pitch in to build arbors with poles and brush under which we could set benches for the revival meetings. We went to Sunday School in the community of Palestine, which is south of Cumby. In addition to the spiritual significance, these church functions served as social gatherings to acquaint all the people within a fairly large area with one another. And, as usual in such an area, everyone knew all of the affairs of everyone else. But it was a wholesome situation, because whenever anyone needed assistance, the word spread quickly, and there were always plenty of helping hands.

Four of us in the area organized the Palestine String Band. Homer Kennedy played the bass violin, Homer Odom played the violin, my younger brother Roy played the piano, and I played the guitar and mandolin. If it had not been for Roy, we could have called ourselves the four Homers! Our most regular job was playing for the only movie house in Sulphur Springs. The movies were silent, and we played to entertain the audience during the intermission while the reels were changed. We also played for many dances in the general area. We were a versatile group. We also sang. For our singing engagements, we were known as the Palestine Quartet. We were on top of the world riding around from one job to another in our rubber-tired buggy pulled by a good looking bay horse.

One Saturday night we played for a dance at Miller Grove, another small community south of Cumby. During the intermission, four or five toughs started a gang fight that almost broke up the dance. After that, we began to slow down some and were more careful when we were asked to play for dances. We were anxious to avoid trouble because we feared that a stigma would develop by association with the rougher element of the population. If that happened and people began to disapprove, parents would not allow their children to attend wherever we played, and we would have been finished for good.

Our farm near Crumby was small, and it was quite a struggle for Dad to make a decent living. When World War I broke out, my oldest brother Ernest tried to enlist in the army, but because of his health he was rejected. I was too young to enlist and, therefore, the war remained far away from us. In 1919, after the war was over, we moved to Durant, Oklahoma, where Dad rented a small farm about half way between Durant and Calera. This farm was larger than the one near Crumby, and we began farming on a larger scale, which meant, of course, more work. In 1920, Dad bought a Fordson tractor. I don't know how we could have gotten along without that machine. As it was, we worked from daylight until dark and managed fairly well. Occasionally, we had some time for fishing or for hunting squirrels or raccoons. Before long, both Ernest and Essie married, and Roy left for school in Norman, Oklahoma, leaving only Reba and me at home. In 1924, I finally tired of the never-ending strenuous work and told Dad I planned to go to Borger, Texas, where I had learned from a cousin, A. O. Pickens, that there were plenty of jobs. Not long after, Dad retired from farming, and my folks moved into the little town of Durant. Before I left home, however, and while we still lived south of Durant, I met a special girl, Edna Burton, who lived at Calera and who later was to become my wife.

In Borger, I found a job with the Phillips Petroleum Company and worked in the oil fields from 1925 to 1927. During this time, Edna and her folks moved to El Centro, California, but she and I continued to grow closer through regular correspondence. Although I had a good boss who treated me well and for whom I worked hard, I disliked the oil field because the people were a rough and rowdy group. It also bothered me that I did not have time to hunt and fish. So, in the spring of 1927, after I received the letter from Albert, I quit the Phillips Company, bought a train ticket and headed for New Mexico hoping to find something that perhaps would be more to my liking. And besides, for the first time I would have the chance to learn more about my older brother.

CHAPTER 3

JOSEPH ALBERT PICKENS (1885-1965)

WHEN ALBERT WROTE and asked me to join him in New Mexico, it was the turning point in my life. He was forty-one years old when I arrived in New Mexico. By then he was an accomplished trapper. I had a lot to learn. I had not been around Albert much, since he was seventeen years my senior. He left home when I was two years old, and when he occasionally came to visit, I, in my youthfulness, was in awe of my worldly half brother.

Albert was born near Cross Timbers, Texas. His mother died when he was six years old. With Lonnie and Albert, our father returned to Hopkins County, east of Black Jack Grove near Cumby. Cotton farming was their livelihood, and in his later years, Albert recalled vividly his first little cotton sack which was made especially for him. It barely touched the ground. He thought picking cotton was fun for a couple of hours, but when the burrs began to stick him and the sun became unbearable, the fun ended. Nevertheless, in the next ten years or so, that little sack was filled many times before the family again moved. Their new home was along Cedar and Schooly Creeks near Palestine, Texas, which is four or five miles south of Cumby. The nearby creeks made life more interesting for Albert, even though there still seemed to be an inexhaustible supply of cotton to be picked. Rabbits, squirrels, raccoons and mink were plentiful, and much to Albert's delight, father bought him a .22 caliber rifle.

Grandmother and Grandfather Pickens, who were well up in their years, lived with them. It was grandpa who first showed Albert the art of making bird traps. Albert caught doves, meadow larks and quail. The quail, which were Bob whites (the only quail in that country), were plentiful in the lush plum and berry thickets. Grandfather taught him to tend his traps often and to pick out and free the young birds. He dropped many a bundle of oats and wheat while trapping birds in those thickets.

To earn Christmas money, Albert had saved up his money to purchase a few steel traps and then proceeded to wreak havoc on the mink and raccoon population. If father did not keep his eye, or perhaps I should say his nose, on Albert, the young man would go off to school wearing what he referred to as his "skunk clothes." Albert did not seem to mind the smell. He observed that girls would "perfume up" and powder their faces, so he reasoned that he could wear a little perfume of his own. He did notice, however, that some of the young ladies avoided him, but he thought they were just being uppity. The skunk hides provided nickels, so he could buy candy anytime. Whenever he did, the girls gathered around, skunk clothes or not. He soon learned the power money can bring to one who possesses it. Lonnie cared little for trapping, so whenever father gave them both a job to do, a dime or quarter could persuade Lonnie to handle it alone.

After Grandmother Pickens died in 1896, grandfather, father and the two boys batched for several years. Albert, because he was the youngest and in his own words, "the most worthless," became the cook, while Dad and Lonnie worked the fields. Albert particularly disliked churning. A two-day supply of cream was enough to provide a good layer for Albert's clothes and enough to make him the hero of the family cat. He claimed that he never did learn to cook, although I was always ready to argue that point.

In his youth, Albert was an active boy, which is another way of saying that on occasion he was a troublemaker. Once during the noon hour at school, Albert and twelve other boys decided to take a swim in a nearby stock tank even though it was strictly forbidden by the teacher. Albert, not knowing the tank was shallow, dived into the water from the dam and buried his head in the mud. By the time he was able to remove enough mud to see, he was late getting back to school. The teacher had learned of the activity, and, because of his standing as a frequent participant in such escapades, Albert was singled out for the initial punishment, known as "britches dusting." The teacher gave him thirteen licks with a hickory switch— one for him and one for each of the other twelve boys. Each of the other lads received only one to three licks apiece. One could have gotten the impression that the Pickens boys made good targets.

Then one day an event occurred that Albert decided was God's blessing to the family. Father married Nancy Belle Jones. Not only did the home brighten, but Albert suddenly was no longer the cook. Free from the burden of kitchen chores, he finally could take his place among the men of the family.

By early 1906, Albert was twenty years old. The family was growing, and the spirit of manhood had been tugging at him for some time. Finally one day he decided he had come of age and announced his intention to drift west to make his own life. Father understood, but with typical parental concern tried gently to dissuade him by telling him that a wandering life would not be easy. Albert, with the typical confidence of youth, was undaunted. In May of that year, with limited funds, he boarded the train at Cumby and headed west. At Sweetwater, Texas, he chopped cotton. In Colorado City he worked as a chore boy on the construction of a large building. Having no trade and because of his size (he weighed 111 pounds at the time), he was limited in the type of work that he could do. But life brightened for him when a man at the hotel where he was boarding offered him a traveling job. Shortly thereafter, he was on his way north with his new boss, Jack Armstead. They followed behind and filled the orders for salesmen who were on the road ahead of them. The job was installing lightning rods, and it was the job Albert had been looking for—he thought.

In 1906, ranches in the panhandle and the Texas plains country were few and far between. Hereford cattle grazed throughout most of the region. Small herds of antelope could be seen racing across the plains. When they first climbed onto the caprock, Albert was impressed by the shallow lakes covered with ducks. In dry years, these lakes are dusty depressions, but 1906 was a wet year, and it was a sight he never forgot.

Albert and Jack worked the entire plains. At that time there was no railroad at Plainview, and only fifteen of the sixty miles of the line from Canyon City to Plainview had been completed. Canyon City was the nearest freight stop, so they were forced to go there for supplies. On one occasion the material that they had ordered had not arrived so they were compelled to wait a week for it.

While they were in Canyon City, on the night of October 21, Carrie A. Nation, the temperance leader, spoke before a capacity audience in front of the court house. Albert was there, and he was to remember her as a great lady who made a thrilling speech. A lifelong teetotaler, he was in those days also disturbed by the number of saloons in the little town. He decided, though, that Carrie A. Nation was wasting her time in Canyon City.

After they replenished their supplies, the pair worked their way eastward and in December arrived at the company headquarters in Oak Cliff, near Dallas. Albert was not too far from home, so he drew his wages and said goodbye to Jack Armstead.

When winter was over he left home again, this time for Vernon, Texas, where he worked for a wheat farmer. In the late fall of 1907, father became ill, and Albert returned home to help on the farm. In June, 1908, he was off again, this time to Sweetwater and on to Comanche and Baylor counties. By the fall of 1909 he was for a while in Haskell, Texas, before moving on to Waxahachie, where he was impressed by a lady streetcar driver who really knew how to handle her black snake whip on the mule teams that pulled her car. He landed a job with the Waxahachie Oil Mill Company. It was at that time that he discovered motion pictures and soon became an ardent moviegoer. His fascination for movies almost cost him his life, though. He somehow became convinced that he could watch movies all day and work and sleep at the same time at night on the job. At the end of a shift early one morning, he sleepily attempted to throw off a short belt, and it caught his arm. When he awoke later, he was told that the short belt had thrown him over the shaft and deposited him on the main belt, which ran across the house. The belt had finally dropped him in a pile of oil cake, bruised but otherwise miraculously unhurt. After mulling over his lifestyle, he decided that city life was too dangerous and once again headed west. He tried Del Rio, Texas, and worked for a man building a railroad grade fifteen miles from town. Within a few days, he came to the conclusion that he had learned all he wanted to about building railroads and left, deciding that if he ever wanted to build his own railroad, he was now well enough qualified. To my knowledge, however, there is no J. A. Pickens Railroad!

On a ranch forty miles north of Del Rio, on the road to Sonora, Albert finally stumbled onto the path that would eventually lead him, and ultimately me, into a lifelong career. For him, the career would fulfill his desire to explore beyond the horizon. This job was to be different from any he had before. The rancher who hired him owned about twelve sections, divided into four pastures, on which he ran sheep and goats. His stock losses to coyotes were enormous, so he offered to pay Albert and outfit him, including steel traps, to combat the predators. Albert began his job in earnest, and very few sheep were killed in the next two years, because he developed into a first-rate trapper.

When the time came to move on again, he ventured into Marathon, Texas, and made two trips into the Big Bend country, helping a county surveyor. From there he journeyed to Midland and then on to Van Horn, where he purchased some gear and headed for the Guadalupe Mountains to try free-lance trapping. In one month he was back in Van Horn to sell eighty furs of coyote, bobcat, gray fox and ringtail cat. It was early 1913. He made a short trip into New Mexico to see the towns of Artesia and Roswell before returning to Motley County to work in the cotton fields in the fall and to trap coyotes in the winter. In the spring of 1914, Albert contracted smallpox, recovered and by summer was on his way with a friend, Lewis Cherry, back to New Mexico. While trapping gray fox and bobcat on the north side of the Capitan Mountains, they also trapped three mountain lions, which was quite an unusual occurrence.

Albert realized that the wild and beautiful country of New Mexico was a place where he could put his talents to work. Besides, the furs he could gather not only would provide him with a means to support himself, but trapping them would also give him a good reason to explore and enjoy this new land. Before the winter of 1914-15 was over, Albert had decided—New Mexico would be his home forever.

Albert and Lewis Cherry crossed the mountains into the small village of Carrizozo, where they met a sheep rancher named J. B. French. It seemed that sheep ranchers in the United States have always had at least one problem in common—coyotes. Mr. French had 8,000 to 10,000 sheep and needed help getting rid of the coyotes. Albert and Cherry went to work for him. After a while, Cherry went back to Texas. Albert stayed on, though, and worked on French's ranch until the fall of 1915, when Charles Moberley, a wolf trapper, came along. Albert joined Moberley in a journey to Silver City, New Mexico, where he began learning the art of trapping wolves. He had good reason: wolves were worth forty dollars apiece, while coyotes and bobcats brought only two dollars each. During that winter and spring they took six wolves and numerous coyotes and bobcats in the lower Black Range country near the N. A. N. ranch on the Mimbres River.

During 1916 and through early 1919, Albert trapped and worked now and then around Carrizozo, Roswell, Las Cruces and Alamogordo. The terrible influenza epidemic of 1918 missed him, but he lost some of his friends.

In his drifting, Albert stopped at the Spur Ranch, hoping to get a job trapping wolves, but found he was too late. J. Stokeley Ligon, the head of predatory animal control in New Mexico for the U. S. Biological Survey, had already sent his top wolf trapper to the ranch. However, Albert's activities had apparently been reported to Ligon. Albert, who was getting his mail at White Tail, New Mexico, on the Mescalero Apache Reservation, received a letter from Ligon offering him a job in Carrizozo. On May 24, 1919, he demonstrated his skills to

JOSEPH ALBERT PICKENS (1885-1965)

E. F. Pope, assistant leader of predatory animal work, and for the next sixteen years, until 1935, he was on the government payroll.

The U. S. Biological Survey assigned him to work in many parts of the state during the years that he was employed by the agency. His first assignment was to trap wolves in the Beaverhead and Slash Ranch country. The owner of Slash Ranch was George W. "Dub" Evans, one of the most prominent cattlemen in southwestern New Mexico. The ranch headquarters was ninety-six miles southwest of Magdalena. Altogether, the ranch covered a total of seventy-one sections of land in the heart of the Gila Wilderness, where some of the best game hunting and fishing in New Mexico could be found. Dub was the son of George Wesley Evans, pioneer West Texas rancher, and Kate Means Evans, whose ranching family become prominent in the oil business in West Texas. Dub's wife was Miss Beulah Gillette of Marfa, Texas, daughter of James B. Gillette, frontiersman and famous early Texas Ranger, about whom many articles and stories have been written. Dub himself was an author and wrote *Slash Ranch Hounds,* published by the University of New Mexico Press in 1951. In his book, Dub makes frequent reference to Albert and his hounds Sam and Nig. Their hunting dogs were a source of great pleasure for Dub and Albert, and both took great pride in their dogs. Dub relates in his book that Albert killed the last lobo wolf in the Black Mountain-Cooney Prairie area, an act for which Dub was immensely grateful because he thoroughly disliked wolves. Dub Evans and his family also became close friends of mine. I spent many memorable days on the trail with him and often visited his home.

The high regard that the ranchers had for Albert cannot be overstated. In 1925, in the area of Fenton's Ranch in the Jemez Mountains northwest of Albuquerque, a mountain lion, given the name of Gray Traveler by some or Rangey by others, acquired a substantial reputation by visiting the farms in the area and wreaking destruction on the domestic stock. The farmers, having neither trained dogs nor traps, were helpless to combat the predators. True to the nature of his breed, Gray

Traveler was seldom seen. With marvelous hearing ability and a keen scent, he invariably spotted the hunters before they saw him and would slink away undetected. Finally, a short while after one of his destructive forays onto one of the farms in the area, the owner, while scouting a nearby cliff, spied his grayish-white head peering down at him. The farmer rode to Fenton's Ranch and reported the lion. Fention immediately invited Albert to come to his ranch to help. When Albert arrived, Fenton joined him, and they set out to find the lion. Almost immediately, they came upon the carcass of Fenton's finest mare. Enraged, Fenton promised Albert all the assistance he could muster to help destroy the killer.

It is the habit of all members of the feline family to claw out a shallow cavity in which to urinate, which they then cover. Mountain lions and lynx cats (bobcats) will commonly cover the spot with pine needles. This scent bed will last for several days and will be examined and often used by every passing lion or cat. Male lions will wander much farther than will females, because lions breed all seasons of the year. The males, when not seeking food are seeking females. Females, being thoroughly familiar with their territory, will visit the "runs" of the males, who in turn revisit the site. When the male discovers the presence of a female, he will trail her until they meet.

Albert was not having much luck finding Gray Traveler. He and his dogs spent several days checking the rims and scanning all the scent stations they could find, but each trail was cold. He knew that the anxiety of the area residents was increasing with each passing day, and he wanted desperately to help. As the word spread farther that Albert had arrived, reports of lion activity began to come in, and Albert set out to investigate each report. During the ensuing six or so weeks, he succeeded in bringing down one half-grown lion, two large females, and captured two kittens, which he sent to Albuquerque. But Old Traveler still eluded him. It was nearing the end of September, and he knew that in this country the cold weather would soon be upon him. The camp would be very uncomfortable, so he started out as early each day as he could.

JOSEPH ALBERT PICKENS (1885-1965)

Finally, on the first of October, shortly after daybreak, the dogs located a scent bed and fresh trail going north. Albert examined the track, and his excitement mounted as he saw that the prints were very large. Perhaps it *was* Gray Traveler! Albert made sure the dogs set out in the direction the lion was moving, because the dogs, when following pad scent, could have just as easily gone the wrong direction and followed the trail backwards. The chase was on! The lion held to the rimrock, as usual, thereby making the trail as difficult as possible. Dogs following the trail will do so by pad scent or body scent. Body scent is short-lasting, and if there is a wind it quickly vanishes. Following pad scent is time-consuming, but with body scent, the dogs can cover a trail much faster.

After following the pad scent for several miles, the dogs came upon the remains of a deer the lion had stalked and killed. The trail was now hot, and the dogs in a frenzy were soon close behind the old lion. They chased him to some sharp bluffs by a river, where he leaped about twenty feet down to a ledge. Here the dogs could not reach him, but at the same time, he could not escape. Albert dismounted and while surveying the situation got his first good look at the lion. It was indeed Gray Traveler! The chase was over. Albert stood and admired the crouching old gray-headed animal, his ears split from combat and his muscle rippling with tremendous power. He estimated the lion to be at least fifteen years old, and it occurred to him that if this marauder had killed a deer, horse or steer once every two days for himself or for his brood, he had slain nearly three thousand head of stock and deer! If half of this kill had been cows, steers and horses worth a low estimate, even in 1925, of twenty-five dollars each, he had destroyed $37,500 worth of livestock. At 1979 values, this figure could easily translate into $200,000. Needless to say, the ranchers and farmers in the area were grateful that Gray Traveler's trail ended for good on the ledge that October day.

In the years that Albert stayed with the Survey, his exploits throughout the state were too numerous to mention. He was variously assigned to areas in Vermejo Park, again in the Cuba country, near Las Vegas, and finally around Chama before he decided to call it quits because he could no longer lift much weight and that was too much of a handicap in the strenuous work for the survey. In Tres Piedras, he bought two homesteads of 160 acres each from Charlie and Marcus Berry, who had settled behind the Tres Piedras ranger station. For the next several years he worked to improve his ranch. During this time he acquired a grazing permit from the government for a piece of land consisting of about 100 acres which was between his two 160-acre tracts and on which stands a large promontory named Pickens Rock, after him. He often worked for Mr. Smith, a rancher in the San Luis Valley of south-Central Colorado who also had a ranch on the Tusas River west of Tres Piedras. Mr. Smith also had a grazing permit for a large area near the Tusas and would drive cattle in from Colorado for summer grazing. Albert worked tending the cattle for Mr. Smith for about ten years. During this time in the winter months, if weather permitted, he would spend as much time trapping as he could.

He developed arthritis, and each winter in the high country became more painful for him. While he loved this area more than any other, in 1945 he decided to leave. He sold his land and moved to Hot Springs, later renamed Truth or Consequences, New Mexico. The warmer climate improved his health, and he worked during the summers of 1947 and 1948 for the New Mexico Department of Game and Fish, trapping coyotes on the Ladder Ranch west of town.

After that, he spent his days fishing on Elephant Butte and Caballo Lakes and lived quietly and peacefully. He died of Cancer on April 11, 1965. Albert's legacy to me was his pride in his work and his commitment to his obligations. He always tried to do his best.

CHAPTER 4

BEN V. LILLY (1856-1936)

AFTER I LEFT Albert in the old mining town of Bland in early June, 1928, my first task for the U. S. Biological Survey was to drive to Roswell in the southeastern part of New Mexico and pick up and deliver some saddle horses to the southwestern part of the state. It occurred to me then that at this pace I would, in a short time, become well acquainted with the entire state. If I had only known.

I was assigned a truck, a Model A ford built for hauling livestock, and had an uneventful trip to Roswell. I picked up the horses and continued my trip to the Beaverhead country west and slightly north of Truth or Consequences. It was in this area that I first met Ben Lilly, perhaps the most famous trapper in the history of the southwestern United States. Mr. Lilly was a fascinating personality. Although he was well along in years when I met him, I became interested in his career and spent time with him whenever I could during the last years of his life.

Ben V. Lilly truly became a legendary figure in his own time. Much has been written on the life and exploits of this unusual man, the last of the mountain men. The most complete account of his life, perhaps a bit too colorful but interesting nevertheless, is *The Ben Lilly Legend,* by J. Frank Dobie. Lilly has been described variously as a woodsman, naturalist and, among other things, a philosopher, but he is best known as a hunter. He spent most of his life hunting, a pursuit which he came to consider his sole mission on this earth.

Benjamin Vernon Lilly was born in Wilcox County, Alabama, on December 31, 1856. Both of his parents were of pioneer stock and native to North Carolina. His mother Margaret Anna McKay, and his father, Albert Lilly, were married on November 27, 1855. Ben was the first born of seven children. Shortly after Ben arrived, the family moved to Kemper County, Mississippi, where the rest of the children were born and where Ben grew to the ripe old age of twelve before he ran away from home. His mother was fairly well educated and insisted that her children also become educated. Ben went back, or was taken home. and was then sent to a military academy in Jackson, Mississippi, but he had little tolerance for schooling. Later, his bachelor uncle Vernon found Ben in Memphis and offered to will to the young man all his property in Louisiana if Ben would settle down and marry. Ben accepted the offer, eventually married in 1880 and had a son who died. He and his wife divorced. He remarried in 1890 and had three more children, including another son, who also died. Through his uncle's will, he gained possession of a farm consisting of three hundred acres of lush bottom land along the Mississippi River.

In the early days when the bottom lands of Louisiana were being settled and including the time that Ben entered the scene, wild game and predators were plentiful. Ben, soon after he arrived on the farm, began to exhibit a yearning to withdraw into solitude by hunting and observing wildlife. As time passed, he developed a distaste for the drudgery of farming. Hunting became an obsession with him and he came to know the woods and canebrakes better than any other man. He became almost a part of the wilderness. He could track any animal anywhere, and incredibly, by some special talent or instinct that few men possess, he always knew where he was. With an unerring sense of direction, he could easily find any location he chose. To appreciate this ability, one must imagine the vast area he roamed, where there were bewildering miles of dense vegetation. Insects, the plague of this land, never seemed to bother him much. Although he did contact malaria, it appeared to have little effect on him. However, he was deaf in one ear, supposedly from sleeping on the wet ground.

His exploits did not escape the attention of the local inhabitants in Louisiana. With each telling, the accounts of his abilities and feats grew until his neighbors began to regard him with awe. The legend had begun.

There is no doubt that Lilly was eccentric. I believe I read somewhere that eccentricity is the stuff that legends are made from, and in Ben Lilly's case, it was certainly true. He had his own code of morality. He was almost fanatic in his convictions. He never touched liquor or tobacco. In fact, he abstained from the use of any stimulant whatsoever, even refusing tea or coffee. He loved wild cherry-leaf tea, usually his only concession to a drink of anything other than water.

Lilly was a pious man. He absolutely refused to perform any task on the Sabbath, no matter how urgent or important it might have been. Once his ox became stuck in a ditch on a Sunday. It had to flounder there until Monday. If Ben was on the trail of a predator on Saturday and could not catch up with it before Sunday, he abandoned the trail until Monday.

One of his most remarkable traits, at least to my way of thinking, because I have spent a great deal of my life on the trail, was that Lilly seldom rode a horse. For him, horses made too much noise and were too visible because of their size. Besides, even though he used hunting dogs, Ben could not scrutinize the ground while on horseback. I find this disdain for the use of horses remarkable, especially for hunting mountain lions. I used dogs and horses for hunting lions, and I can say from experience that the effort involved, even on horseback, demands exertion that can tire any man beyond what he ever imagined he could endure. And Lilly did it on foot! Almost without exception he went everywhere on foot. He was once invited to attend and speak before an annual convention of the Texas and Southwestern Cattle Growers Association held in El Paso. At the time, Lilly was living and hunting in the Black Range area of southwestern New Mexico. Victor Culberson, a well known Grant County cattleman and head of the GOS Cattle Company, asked Lilly to speak on his experience as a predatory animal hunter. Lilly accepted and immediately set out on foot for El Paso. He made it to Hurley before some of the GOS ranch hands in an auto overtook him and persuaded him to travel with them to El Paso. It was not easy to persuade him, though, because riding in an auto nauseated him. Lilly was quoted as saying as he entered the car, "My, my, you've spoiled my trip. I was just going to have a nice little walk down to El Paso." El Paso is roughly eighty miles from the GOS headquarters.

Largely due to Lilly's efforts, the predator population in Louisiana diminished to the point that there was no longer the threat there had once been. But by this time hunting had become an obsession with him. His second wife, Mary had also become obsessed—with putting an end to his long forays into the canebrakes. However, it was not to be. No one knows for sure why the break between the two finally came about. It may have been that he just decided that in order to continue hunting he would have to find another place where animals were plentiful and where his special talents could be useful. It could also have been that Mary told Ben if he ever went on another hunt for all she cared he could keep going! In 1901, he did just that, and he never went back. There is plenty of evidence, though, that he loved his family. Before he left home, he transferred all of his property to Mary. So long as he was able, he also faithfully sent home checks from his earnings for killing predatory animals. The stockmen paid a bounty on stock-killing bear, lions and wolves.

He slowly drifted westward. While in Texas in 1907, he received a telegram which summoned him to President Theodore Roosevelt's hunting camp on Tensas Bayou. The president wanted to kill a bear, and his aides went all out to enlist all the help available. After almost two weeks, Teddy finally got his bear, but Lilly did not share in the glory. While the big party was finishing the hunt, Lilly, being too much of a loner to want to be in on that, was off by himself looking for fresh signs. Two men from Mississippi were given credit for chasing down the bear for the president.

From Texas, Lilly wandered across the border into Mexico at Eagle Pass and on into the Santa Rosa Mountains in the northern part of Coahuila. It was 1908. He worked his way towards Chihuahua and beyond for two years, while supplying fresh-killed game for miners and ranchers. He admired that country greatly and often spoke fondly of it in his later years. The Madero Revolution made it difficult for him to obtain ammunition, but he managed to continue his trek westward for another year before he finally reentered the United States in the southwestern corner of New Mexico.

Lilly was fifty-five when he found the area where he could be content to spend the remainder of his days. The ranchers in southwestern New Mexico were desperate and had asked for federal aid to stop the wolves, grizzly bears and mountain lions that were devastating twenty percent of their stock each year. The situation was tailor-made for Lilly. He worked for a while for the U. S. Forest Service, collecting an occasional bonus from a grateful rancher to supplement his salary of seventy-five dollars per month. For the first time in his life, he was a financial success.

Part of the area that he hunted and roamed is called the Gila Wilderness area, so decreed by Theodore Roosevelt: the first area to be designated as a wilderness in the United States by Aldo Leopold. In addition to the Gila Wilderness, Lilly also hunted the Black Range for a combined area of three-fourths of a million acres. The high mountains of the Black Range can be bitter cold in the winter, a condition unfamiliar to a man from the swamps of Louisiana. But he hardly seemed to notice. Besides, nothing could deter him from his mission.

Wherever he was, whenever night overtook him he camped. He carried only a small backpack containing a frying pan, a bag of salt, cornmeal, or sometimes rice, and a small tin pail in which he brewed his cherished cherry-leaf tea. He also carried extra cartridges in a tobacco sack and a stout axe. He had long ago adapted to the hearing loss he developed in Louisiana, and the adaptation had become his trademark. When hunting, he kept two of his ever present dogs on a leash that he fastened to his belt, and they became his ears. He also relied on their keen sense of scent to hold the trail of a lion or bear.

Lilly was one of the first employees of the U. S. Biological

Survey in New Mexico. He began with the survey in 1916, and was in its employ off and on for several years. He was working for the government when I first met him in 1928. I was assigned to transport two saddle horses and one pack horse from Roswell to the Beaverhead country. It took me two days to make a trip which these days would take probably about a half a day, but I had to take a more roundabout route than would be necessary today. I spent the first night in Socorro at the School of Mines, where they had a corral for the horses. I then traveled south from Magdalena through Beaverhead to the Diamond Bar Ranch, where I met Lilly. He had his hounds with him and was hunting and doing well. Not only was he on the payroll of the survey, but he was still being paid a bounty by the ranchers for mountain lions and grizzly bears that were destroying livestock in the area.

By 1934, Lilly was seventy-eight years old and was beginning to show his age. He was staying at the GOS Ranch, but was not able to do much. He hunted some and puttered around the ranch, but his health declined and the ranchers decided to take him to the county home, known as the County Farm, on the Big Dry Creek south of Glenwood. At that time, I had left the employ of the survey and had been working for the New Mexico Department of Game and Fish for about three years. I had been transferred to Silver City, in the southwestern part of the state. I often stopped at the county home and visited with Lilly. With each visit it was noticeable that his mind was gradually failing. I recall on one visit to the home, Mrs. Harry Hines, the manager, permitted me to walk around with him. After a while we sat under the shade of a tree, and he told me, "If you want to catch turkeys, you want to trail a turkey until you know his habits, then you act like one, and be one." The statement at the time seemed to me to be perhaps a bit senile, but as I have thought about it over the years, I have come to realize that probably that bit of advice summed up the secret of his success as a hunter. I believe that he studied the habits of all the animals so carefully that he not only knew everything they would do in any situation, but he could predict their moves before they made them. Perhaps he did learn to think as the animals did. After all, they shared the same environment—the same home.

I never was privileged to hunt with him. However, my half brother Albert did, and I have often wished that I could have too. Ben Lilly spent his last days at the home south of Glenwood, where he died quietly on December 17, 1936.

A magnificent portrait, a full length canvas of Lilly, was painted in 1922 by "Buck" Dunton, famous artist of the southwest who lived in Taos, New Mexico. The portrait was exhibited in the National Academy of Design in New York City, where it received wide acclaim.

In 1941, T. Y. Harp, a friend of Lilly's in his youth in the canebrakes of Louisiana, proposed a memorial marker to Lilly. The plan was interrupted by World War II, but was revived in 1946. Donations were received from friends in a half dozen states. Active in the plan with Harp were Fred Winn, who once supervised the Gila Forest; J. Stokely Ligon of the U. S. Biolocigal Survey, who was not only Lilly's supervisor, but also his highly regarded friend; Monroe H. Goode of Fort Worth, Texas; J. Frank Dobie, the novelist and historian who probably did more to perpetuate the memory of Lilly than anyone else; Melvin Porterfield of Silver City; and W. H. McFadden of Fort Worth, Texas, for whom Lilly often acted as guide on hunting trips. The memorial was cast in bronze and was erected in 1947 at the entrance to the Gila Wilderness area north of Silver City. The marker reads:

1856—BEN V. LILLY—1936

Born in Alabama and reared in Mississippi, BEN V. LILLY in early life was farmer and trader in Louisiana, but turned to hunting of panthers and bears with a passion that led him out of swamps and canebrakes, across Texas, to tramp the wildest mountains of Mexico, and finally become a legendary figure and dean of wilderness hunters in the southwest. He was a philosopher, keen observer, naturalist, a cherisher of good hounds, a relier of his rifle, and a handicraftsman in horn and steel. He loved little children and vast solitudes. He was a pious man of singular honesty and fidelity and a strict observer of the sabbath. New Mexico mountains were his final hunting range and the charms of the Gila Wilderness held him to the end.

Erected 1947, By Friends

CHAPTER 5

EDNA BURTON BECOMES MRS. HOMER PICKENS

AFTER MY FIRST visit to the Beaverhead country, where I met Ben Lilly, I drove back to Albuquerque and met Lee English, who was to be my next immediate supervisor. Lee also worked under A. E. Gray in predatory animal and rodent control. At that time, his assignment was project leader in the plains county of De Baca, Curry, Chaves and Roosevelt counties in the east-central part of the state. I was impressed with Lee. In 1928 he was forty years old. He was tall, about six-two, and well built, carrying about 180 pounds. His reddish complexion matched his fiery red hair, but not his temperament. Lee and his wife Mamie were two of the most pleasant people I ever met. They are now both deceased, but I shall always cherish the time and friendship that we shared.

On our way to Fort Sumner, the project headquarters, Lee explained to me that during the summer months, the U. S. Biological Survey concentrated its manpower on prairie dog control. Winter months were the time for coyote control. I had wondered earlier how prairie dogs could be such a problem that the big United States government would spend its money to mobilize experts against these little creatures. I soon learned that small as they might be, collectively they were a very serious problem to ranchers. In this land where natural feed for cattle is sparse, eight prairie dogs will destroy the grass on enough land to feed one cow. Thousands of prairie dogs on the increase can produce disasterous results where human livelihood depends on cattle and sheep. In a near panic, ranchers were asking for help, and the survey responded by sending several teams into the region to control the prairie dog population explosion.

Lee and I spent the remainder of the summer ranging several miles in every direction, reducing the numbers of the little rodents wherever we found them. It was during one of these sojourns that I saw my first black-footed ferret, a shy little creature seldom seen by man and now on the endangered species list.

On a warm day in August, as we were about to complete our season's work, Lee and I returned to Fort Sumner for the few supplies we needed for one more week's work. In town we met Ross Wilmeth and his assistant, A. H. Riley, both also survey employees. During the course of our conversation, Ross suggested that we hurry our purchases so we could have a little extra time to join them in having a bowl of chili and a mug of home brew at the Pecos River Bridge Cafe. The cafe was located at the west end of the old wooden bridge and was operated by Deluvina Maxwell. She was recorded by several authors to be the sweetheart of Billy the Kid at the time he was killed on June 21, 1881, by Pat Garrett in Pete Maxwell's house in Fort Sumner. It is popularly believed that the Kid had gone to Fort Sumner to be with Deluvina and, in doing so, had sealed his fate. As we entered the cafe, I noticed that it was almost completely dark inside. The only light came from coal oil lamps and a few candles scattered about the room. Deluvina, who appeared to be in her middle sixties, had been married many years, had a family and appeared to be somewhat shy at first. Perhaps because the light was poor, she was slow to recognize Lee, who had worked around the area for years, but when she did recognize him, she immediately became friendly and cordial. We ordered the speciality (and only choice) of the house, chili and beer, and when I took my first bite of the famous New Mexican dish, I was instantly afraid that I had just made the biggest mistake of my life. I reached for the beer, but because of my tears and the poor light, I had to grope around a bit. I nearly panicked before I finally found the beer and succeeded in cooling the fire. The so-called mugs

EDNA BURTON BECOMES MRS. HOMER PICKENS

I remember well. They were made from large tomato juice cans. Wire was wrapped around the top and bottom and then twisted together to form the handle. The beer was somewhat bitter, but it was a lifesaver!

In late September I was informed that I would be promoted to predator control project leader and would be stationed in Roswell, on the Pecos River south of Ft. Sumner. Along with the promotion would come another raise, and I would be making one hundred and five dollars per month! I was elated, because with my new station and affluency, I could now make plans for getting married. It was a happy prospect for me, and the world brightened considerably that day.

I reported to my new job and for the first time was given an assistant. The principal problem area was within the land owned by Jess Corn, who lived on Salt Creek Ranch, twenty miles north of Roswell in Chaves County. Jess was thirty years old when we first met, and he became a valued friend of mine throughout the remainder of his life. His ranch north of Roswell included over fifty-four sections of fine grazing land. He also owned another thirty-eight sections in the Huggins area, eighty miles north of Roswell. He raised an average of over fifteen hundred head of thoroughbred Hereford cattle and five thousand head of purebred Ramboulett sheep on one of the most improved ranches in the state. But Jess had a problem. With all those fine sheep, the coyotes found his land to be ideal feeding grounds. The wily canine flourished—at the expense of Jess. The Survey answered Jess's call for help by sending me to his and other ranches, where I worked throughout the winter of 1928-29 trapping coyotes.

One evening as I was returning to the Corn Ranch and riding one of Jess's two-year-old mares, I allowed the horse to get too close to the "wolf-proof" fence, and the toe of my right boot caught in one of the small openings in the fence. My boot heel was jerked inward, causing me to dig the rowel of my spur into the horse's flank. The animal reacted instantly and bucked. My boot was still caught in the fence, and a searing pain convinced me that my leg was being torn off. It is amazing what punishment the human body can endure, because as I lay on the ground, I could hardly believe my leg was still attached. However, it really was still there—unbroken even—but it was extremely painful for several days while I limped around. Those "wolf-proof" fences, incidentally, were wire woven, with openings that were small enough to prevent a coyote from getting through. They were expensive, especially considering the amount required to protect sheep numbering in the thousands. The cost of the fence was an indication of the price the ranchers were willing to pay to keep the coyotes from their stock. I also protected the antelope herds that ranged that vast, open range.

When the spring of 1929 arrived, I was assigned once again to rodent control. During the next few months, throughout the summer and into fall, I worked in the Beaverhead country, the Vermejo Park area of northeastern New Mexico and in the Chama area before returning again to Roswell.

Roswell was an interesting place in 1928-29. Most of the people in the vicinity were ranchers and the businessmen in town were generally connected in some way with ranching. It was a small town with a population of about five to seven thousand people. Abundant vegetables and fruit were grown in the Hondo valley west of town. It was an energetic place, and with the New Mexico Military School well established, the town appeared to have no limit to future growth and prosperity.

Cowboys in those days, like cowboys before them, led a rough and demanding life, and it was not unusual for one of these range riders to let off a little steam on occasion. Whenever one of these high-spirited cowboys drank too heavily and found it difficult to walk—he rode. On two separate occasions while I was in Roswell, the town barbers bore the brunt of this quirk when cowboys under the influence decided they needed a haircut. Each time, the cowboys rode right through the front door, scattering customers and barbers. But it was a cattle town, and no one really seemed to mind, even the barbers.

By the fall of 1929, I was making one hundred and twenty dollars per month, and I decided the time was right. I asked for

EDNA BURTON BECOMES
MRS. HOMER PICKENS

a few days off and went to Albuquerque, where for $850, I bought a brand new 1930 Chevrolet coupe from Clyde Oden. In my new car, I left for El Centro, California, to ask Edna to marry me. I was elated when she accepted my proposal. We decided that we would make our plans, set the date by correspondence as soon as possible, and meet in Phoenix, Arizona, for our marriage. When I returned to Albuquerque, I asked John Gatlin for time off to get married. John was hesitant because he was not too eager to spare me, even for my marriage. He finally acquiesced, however, and made me a happy man.

On the morning of January 7, 1930, we arrived at the courthouse in Phoenix. Edna, who had arrived by auto with her brother and his wife, looked splendid in a long blue crepe dress and blue shoes. A neighbor of her sister-in-law had made a little hat of gold lace, which fit snugly on her head. I wore a light navy blue suit with a cutaway vest and bell-bottom trousers from Globe Tailors in Albuquerque. The material was a sort of basket weave and tightly woven. The clerk who gave us our license began kidding me for having come all the way from Roswell to get married, so in good nature I returned the kidding—much to Edna's chagrin. Before the clerk finally led us to the district judge's chamber, she was fuming. The final blow came when we stood before the judge, who in a most undignified manner spoke about ten words and then said, "That'll be ten dollars and she's yours." I handed him a twenty dollar bill and said, "See if you can make ten dollars out of that," meaning "Give me my change." He did, and she was mine at long last.

Edna's brother took us to dinner, and we spent the night in Phoenix. The next morning Edna's brother and his wife left for El Centro, and we left for Roswell. The trip took two days. We spent the second night in Gila Bend, Arizona.

Tanner's Apartments was the only apartment housing in Roswell, so naturally, it was our first domicile. Ours was a small apartment with a living room complete with a drop-leaf table, one bedroom and a small kitchen. We shared the bathroom with the next apartment. The rent was thirty dollars per month. We stayed just one month, though, because we were informed that the rent was to increase. Edna decided that not only was the rent too high, but the days were too lonely, so she announced that she would be moving out into the field and into my tent, where we would share the wide open spaces together. I did not know what to make of this and had no idea whether or not it would work, but she was determined. As it turned out, those were some of the happiest days of our lives. We spent twenty dollars per month on groceries and had one hundred dollars per month left that we could spend or save as we wished.

When spring came we began to move around. The survey sent us north on rodent control. Edna decided that so long as she was in camp she might as well work for the survey also, so when the opportunity arose, she approached manager Tom Talley on the subject. To our surprise (especially mine) A. E. Gray and John Gatlin liked the idea. She was hired. She helped me load and haul the poison and equipment and joined me in the field. The work of scattering the poison grain was all done on horseback. We moved into the area near El Rito, Canjilon, Española, and finally to Vermejo Park, where I met Elliott Barker and where the next important phase of my life would begin.

During our travels from Roswell to Vermejo Park, Edna and I spent many happy hours sitting before the campfire making plans and talking about the past. New Mexico, or at least part of it, was no stranger to her. As a youngster she had lived near Tucumcari, New Mexico, close to the Texas line. The population in that area was sparse then and in that respect has not changed much compared to the rest of New Mexico even today.

CHAPTER 6

EDNA BURTON PICKENS

IN 1906, NEW MEXICO was still a territory and was not destined to become the forty-seventh state of the Union for six more years. The east-central part of the state was sparsely settled when the federal government made homestead tracts available for anyone willing to move in. Edna's parents were living in Oklahoma at the time and were among those who decided to become pioneers. With Edna, who was one year old at that time, her older brother Finis, and the family belongings tucked into a covered wagon, the Burtons traveled across the plains of the Texas Panhandle and settled on the plains of east-central New Mexico, four miles from Norton, near Tucumcari.

On the land they selected, her father made a dugout for the family dwelling. This type of structure was common in those days. Building materials were scarce and costly. To construct the dugout, he excavated to a depth of about five feet. From ground level upwards he erected walls that were topped by a slanted metal roof. Steps cut into the ground led down into the dugout. Edna recalls that there was a small window near the cook stove where her mother kept a bowl of everlasting yeast. Mrs. Burton did not make fresh bread every day, so the yeast would dry and would keep for a long time. Whenever she was ready to make bread she added warm water to the yeast, and it was ready. The dugout was heated by a corner fireplace. The rear of the dwelling had a larger window, and the family's big yellow cat, Lippo, entered and left the house through the window. Mrs. Burton kept her trunk containing extra bedding under the window and always left the lid open so the cat could have a soft place to land. The cat's name came from an article in a magazine sent from Oklahoma by one of Mrs. Burton's sisters. The only written news about the outside world came from those magazines, the most popular being the *Ladies Home Journal*. The only other reading material they had was the family Bible, which no family was without and which in many ways helped the homesteaders to survive.

The only income the family had came from Mr. Burton's trips to Kansas to work during the harvest season. Whenever he returned he would hitch the team to the wagon and drive to Tucumcari, seventeen miles from home, to buy supplies. Sugar, flour, beans and potatoes came in one hundred pound sacks. Salt, coffee and lard came in twenty-five pound cans. The only fruits available—peaches, apples, prunes, apricots and raisins—were always dried.

In order to farm the land, the mesquite had to be cleared. While Edna's father was away, her mother and brother cleared what they could, but it was slow work and in the six years they were there, they made scant headway on the 160-acre tract. They did manage to have a small garden, however.

They had no well, so water had to come from a spring that was one and a half miles from the house. The water was hauled in four barrels on a flatbed wagon pulled by Maude, the family mule. On the way home from the spring it was necessary to cross an arroyo, and each time, old Maude would balk at having to pull the heavy load through the sand. The first time it happened, Mrs. Burton dipped about half the water from each barrel and poured it onto the ground. The mule was satisfied and proceeded. The next time, Maude was too impatient to wait for all that water to be poured out and started on across. Mrs. Burton took her cue, and from then on whenever Maude would balk at the arroyo, she would slowly pour out one bucket of water and Maude would then proceed.

Life on the farm always provides chores for the kids, but there was one chore that was somewhat unusual for Edna and Finis. They had to milk a goat. A cow would have been preferred, but the family could not afford one. As it was, having the goat was much more logical since it ate mesquite and other dry climate vegetation that a cow would not touch. The goat, however, could be a real nuisance. It would get up on the slanted metal roof of the dugout, and try as they might, they could not keep it off. The kids thought it funny, but their parents failed to see the humor in the loud clatter of little hoofs across the roof at night.

Rattlesnakes, centipedes and prairie dogs were plentiful. Somehow the kids failed to appreciate the danger of the snakes. Often, lacking anything else to do, they amused themselves by joining their little dog, Spot, in "fighting" rattlesnakes. After they located a coiled snake, they approached it like true little matadors. Finis would hit it with a rock, and when it uncoiled they took turns darting in to retrieve the rock. Spot did his share of antagonizing the snake by staying a respectable distance and barking his tiny heart out. When the snake finally decided it could not win the game, it would slip into a prairie dog hole, and the kids would have to go find another one. Sometimes they would just give up and go look for their friend, a little sheepherder who lived nearby.

Ned Folks, a young Spanish-American sheepherder, was their every day friend—and their tutor. He taught both of them Spanish, and before long they were fairly proficient in their new tongue. In return, they helped Ned with his English. One word he never could master, though, was "ashes." The way it came out when he first tried it embarassed him, and he refused to say the word after that.

The west, it seemed, was never really settled until the women arrived. They were the stabilizing influence that was needed and often needed badly. By the early 1900's, the Tucumcari area was pretty well civilized. It had become that way because of women such as Mrs. Burton and her friends, and they meant to keep it civilized. The women would get together and form Bible study groups. Such groups were not only important to the parents, but they also served as an important facet in the upbringing of their children. The Bible studies were taken extremely seriously. The groups met alternately in different homes, and each person attending wore his or her finest clothes.

Edna's dresses were made from dyed Diamond flour sacks that were sent to her mother by Edna's aunts. The aunts also sent shoes and old coats. The shoes were worn only during cold weather, however. Mrs. Burton altered the coats for the children. Aunt Ann and Aunt Lizzie and her husband, Uncle Walter, visited New Mexico and the Burtons once. They came by train. Uncle Walter worked for the Missouri, Kansas and Texas Railroad and had passes. As a gift, they brought Mrs. Burton a sewing machine, which she thereafter put to good use in keeping the children well dressed.

One evening after the wind had been blowing fiercely all day, it suddenly stopped and became disturbingly quiet. The sunset was beautiful. Then a black cloud appeared on the horizon with a tail long enough to touch the ground. As suddenly as it had stopped, the wind began to howl again. The children climbed onto the roof of the dugout to watch as the funnel, fortunately, moved away. Mrs. Burton ordered them into the house just before the downpour began. Sometime during the night the rain finally stopped, and they all awoke the next morning to a beautiful new day. The storm had gone.

Edna was four years old when Clifford was born. He was never a healthy child. Edna took care of him while Mrs. Burton and Finis continued to try to clear the mesquite. They had no baby bottles or nipples, so Edna had to feed him milk with a spoon, which usually quieted him.

When Edna was six, Mr. Burton became ill and was unable to follow the harvest. The family had to struggle to survive that winter, and the hardship convinced the Burtons that they must return to Oklahoma, where they could get help. The first obstacle they had to overcome was a lack of money for the trip. They had none. Edna and Finis became the providers. Using all the tricks they had learned in their games, they caught twelve cottontail rabbits. Since rabbits and rattlesnakes both used prairie dog holes, the children had to fight a few rattlesnakes in the process—only this time it was no game. They had no gun, so they had to kill the rabbits with a rock. They used a wire to twist into the rabbits' skin in order to pull them from the holes. Their parents skinned the animals and put them in a tub of cold fresh water. Mr. Burton then delivered them to Tucumcari in a canvas-covered tub and went from house to house selling them. The sale provided just enough cash for them to begin their trip.

Edna and Finis continued to attend school until they were ready to leave New Mexico. Edna was promoted to the second grade and Finis to the fifth. Both developed a cough, and it was discovered that every one in school had whooping cough, including them. The two children brought it home to Clifford, adding to the family's troubles. Edna and Finis recovered quickly, but the disease was especially hard on baby Clifford. Even though Mr. Burton's illness was worse and the baby was ill, there was no alternative; they packed and left.

Edna and Finis played along the way. Whenever they found a tree, the two older children sat in the shade and talked until the wagon was out of sight, then ran to catch up to it. Displaying ingenuity, they invented a game whereby they grabbed two spokes of a wagon wheel and put their feet inside the wheel rim. By stiffening their bodies, they competed to see how many times they could go around as the wagon rolled along. When they let loose they tried to pick a smooth place to land, but more often than not they landed in stickers instead. Somehow, neither got hurt, but Edna's long braids became more dirt than hair! Fortunately, the family usually found water where they could stop for the night, and while their parents made camp and prepared the meal, the kids continued their youthful frolicking.

One day they had to stop early because Mr. Burton's condition worsened. Fortunately, they found a particularly good place to camp. It was about May or June, 1912. After they had been in camp for a while, they looked up and spied a large black woman holding a baby on her hip with one hand and carrying a bucket in the other one. Following behind her were six or eight more kids. Edna and Finis, pleased to have found some playmates, started to run to meet the group, but Mrs. Burton stopped them. She went out to meet the woman and explained to her that the Burtons had whooping cough and she did not want that large group of children to catch it. The woman, in appreciation for Mrs. Burton's concern, handed her the bucket, which was full of fresh milk. Mrs. Burton graciously accepted the bucket and took it back to the wagon where she transferred the milk to a crock. Mr. Burton put a plate on the crock and set it in the stream while his wife returned the bucket. When she returned it, the black woman told her some interesting news about the sinking of the Titanic with all those rich folks aboard. She said, "Jes think about John Jacob Astor gwine down on that ship with all that money." She told Mrs. Burton that she was not sure when it had happened, because news traveled slowly in those days. Later, while they were enjoying every drop of the milk, the Burtons explained to their children that Mr. Astor did not take all of his money with him to the bottom of the ocean!

They finally made it safely back to Oklahoma to their aunt and uncle's house. Clifford did finally recover in about a year, but Mr. Burton died soon after they arrived, leaving Mrs. Burton with the difficult responsibility of raising the three children by herself. Uncle Walter, who had a blacksmith shop, taught Finis the trade. He also taught him mechanics, which became increasingly more useful as Henry Ford's automobiles began to swarm over the nation.

During the next few years as the children grew, Mrs. Burton worked as a midwife and at other jobs she could find. The children also worked, and with the generous help of their relatives, they made it through those difficult times.

In 1925, Edna graduated from high school, and even completed one semester at Southwestern College at Durant, Oklahoma. She was twenty years old and was working for the bank when we met. I had been in town and was on my way home. My cousin Orville and I were stopped on the road because of a washed-out bridge, when Edna and two of her friends came along, having just left a movie in town. Edna's friend, Ira Sharp, introduced us, and soon afterwards the courtship began and blossomed.

When I left for Borger, Texas, she went to Wetumka,

Oklahoma, and worked as a PBX operator for the Phillips Petroleum Company. By this time, Finis was married and had moved to El Centro, California. Mrs. Burton, Edna, and Clifford all wanted to visit Finis and his wife, so they left for California. They decided to stay in El Centro, and Edna worked for a dime store there until she joined me in Phoenix where we were married.

I asked Edna to give me her impression of our first year together, and what she had to say is best repeated in her own words.

"Homer rented a nice apartment for me in Roswell, but he had to be gone for two weeks. A few people in the apartment house were friendly, but I was still lonely. I spent the first days arranging the apartment, and then I read a lot and wrote letters. When Homer came back after the two weeks, I had already had enough. I told him I wanted to go to camp with him. The apartment was paid up two months in advance, but Homer said I could go out to his camp for the following weekend. I was to travel a certain highway twelve miles and go through a gate on the left. From that point on he would tie red rags on bushes the remainder of the way to his tent. When Friday came, I found the camp all right, but on Sunday I had to return to town to the apartment. I told Homer then that when the rent was up I was going to live in the tent with him. He said he had to obtain permission for that, so he asked, and it was granted. I went to live with him in camp, and from then on when we moved around I drove our car and he drove a government truck, in which he hauled tents and his equipment. He also pulled a trailer for his horse.

"With this living arrangement, we were together, and we also saved money. But, at times, living in that tent was miserable. While we were in the Roswell country, our tents would nearly blow away in the terrible winds. When we left the Roswell area, life improved. We were sent to an area north of Albuquerque and finally to Vermejo Park, the most beautiful place in the world. Getting into Vermejo Park country was quite a chore because the roads, if you could call them that, were extremely rough. But it was worth it. After we arrived,

I had a strange reaction. The high altitude made me sleepy. I was groggy for weeks before I finally adjusted. While there we met Mr. and Mrs. Elliott Barker. Mrs. Barker is a lovely sweet person and was very kind to me, helping me in every way she could.

"Whenever I would get tired and lonely from staying in camp, I would ride with the crew. Homer would always hang a bag of poisoned grain on my saddle horn, and I would work along with the others horseback. It occurred to me one day that I was doing for free what the school boys were being paid thirty dollars per month to do. So without hesitation, I expressed my view to Homer, and he replied, 'If you've got nerve enough to ask Tom Talley for a job, okay.' A few days later, Mr. Talley visited our camp, so I asked him for a job—and he told Homer to put me on the payroll! From then on, I worked every day. I consider it one of the most enjoyable times of my life. We still call that summer our honeymoon."

CHAPTER 7

VERMEJO PARK

THE HISTORY OF the Vermejo Park Ranch is fascinating, and perhaps someday someone will write a book about its development.

The ranch was part of the original Maxwell Land Grant that Lucien Bonaparte Maxwell put together. In 1844, Maxwell, a trapper who had migrated to Taos, married Luz Beaubien, daughter of Don Carlos Beaubien, who came from Canada in 1823. Carlos Beaubien and Guadalupe Miranda had been awarded a sizable land grant by Mexican Governor Manuel Armijo on the east side of the Sangre de Cristo Mountains in 1841. The grant contained possibly 32,000 to 97,000 acres at that time. In 1847, shortly after General Stephen Watts Kearny's "Army of the West" took New Mexico from Mexico, Maxwell began constructing buildings at Rayado, and ten years later he began the town of Cimarron.

There has been much controversy in the courts and in history books about what transpired next concerning the grant boundaries. Maxwell, through a series of shrewd moves, began acquiring the remaining interest in the grant. Possibly by assisting government land surveyors in pointing out natural land markers, he expanded the acreage to a staggering 1,714,-764.93 acres. It was and is the largest single tract ever owned in the United States by an individual. Oddly enough, no one contested his ownership until about 1868, when word filtered out that gold had been discovered in Moreno Valley, well known now for Eagle Nest Lake and Angel Fire. The discovery led to increasing problems, and when various parties began showing an interest in the grant, Maxwell decided to sell.

Supposedly, he eventually received $650,000 for his holdings and invested $150,000 in the First National Bank of Santa Fé. He lost nearly all of this, and finally sold his interest to Stephen Benton Elkins and Thomas Benton Catron, who had opened a rival bank. In the meantime, he had moved to Fort Sumner, where he established a ranch that was not particularly successful, perhaps because his heart was never in Fort Sumner. He died moderately wealthy on July 25, 1875. Slightly less than six years later, Billy the Kid was killed by Pat Garrett in one of the Maxwell bedrooms, and was buried in the same cemetery as Lucien Maxwell.

At least part of the land that would become the Vermejo Park Ranch was sold by Maxwell in 1870 to a Dutch Company, which later formed the Maxwell Cattle Company. Frank Springer was hired as the company attorney. The Springers would eventually become one of the most powerful and respected families in New Mexico. The United States Congress passed a law prohibiting aliens from acquiring territorial land and barred corporations from acquiring more than 5,000 acres. The Dutch Company was forced to realign, and it elected a syndicate composed mainly of Americans to conduct the company's affairs.

In an important decision the U. S. Supreme Court recognized the Maxwell Land Grant Company's title to the Grant. It was a terrible blow to settlers in the area, who had hoped to win the right to stay. Many of these had settled along Vermejo Creek. Tempers flared as the company attempted to gain control of the property. The Colfax County War broke out, and it was not until the summer of 1900 that open hostilities finally ceased. It has been said that the bitterness has never died and persists to this day.

The ranch was purchased by William H. Bartlett, who set about constructing one of the most beautiful ranches in the southwest. The main buildings were three magnificent redstone mansions, which when I first saw them in 1928 were called the "big houses." Two of the homes were for his sons and the largest he built for himself. It had thirty-one guest rooms, seven baths and several showers. I often heard it referred to as Roff House. It burned in the late forties and was not rebuilt. There were a large hot house to supply flowers the year around, a palm house, a tennis court, a wine cellar and four cottages for the estate's personnel. The lawn in front of the houses was five acres and was enclosed by a high rock wall. Deer often came in to graze on the lawn. Nearby were a dairy barn and a general store. About two miles north of the mansion were several cattle corrals. A huge bunkhouse and commissary for the cowboys and a big home for the cattle foreman were situated near the corrals. Vermejo Creek supplied irrigation water for miles of grain fields and alfalfa. Cowboys working on the west side of the ranch had to travel twenty-five miles east for their supplies.

When I first arrived on the ranch, it was owned by the Vermejo Club, a Delaware Corporation which had purchased the property from the widow of the youngest son, the last of the Bartletts, who died in 1920. The Corporation turned the ranch into a playground for its famous members, among whom were Cecil B. de Mille, Harvey Firestone, Max C. Fleischmann, and F. W. Kellogg. I personally met Charlie Chaplin, Will H. Hayes, Douglas Fairbanks, and Tom Mix. There were over a hundred other members, all well known in their day, who paid $1,000 yearly membership fees.

In 1928 my job with the U. S. Biological Survey was to poison prairie dogs on the 750,000 acre ranch, then managed by Tom Talley. I slowly worked my way around the ranch with a crew of high school students and worn-out cowboys, a chuck wagon pulled by a team, and a cook named Colorado. We used about forty-five head in that job, and the cowboys called it the horse remuda.

CHAPTER 8

EARLY DAYS IN THE GAME AND FISH DEPARTMENT

ON MAY 6, 1931, I became the first person to receive an appointment from the New Mexico Game and Fish Department under the leadership of State Game Warden Elliott Barker. In my new job I made $135 per month, five dollars per month more than I had made with the U. S. Biological Survey. In those days, there were only a few employees in the department, and each employee had to stand ready to handle any job that might come along. And because there were so few of us we had to cover large areas of the state. Each of us was responsible for thousands of square miles. My first assignment when I reported for work in Albuquerque, where I spent several weeks, was familiarizing myself with departmental procedures. When this period was over, I was assigned primarily as trapper and patrolman but also as a hunter and public relations officer covering the northeastern quarter of the state. My headquarters would be in Las Vegas.

Las Vegas in 1931 was, I decided, still another contrast. The town had a problem—and I suppose it still does. It is not a problem that in the early days of the community was unique in the southwest. It is just that Las Vegas has hung on to its problem longer than most towns.

Las Vegas is not one town, it is two. The division came about in 1881 when the first railroad came into New Mexico from Colorado across Raton Pass. The community division in Las Vegas was the first such occurence in New Mexico, but it would not be the last. Landowners with property near the established town tried to make the most of the railroad's coming in and held out for what they hoped to be handsome profit. The railroad company balked and simply bought cheaper land farther east and built a depot and roundhouse. The merchantile houses of Otero and Sellers (later to become Gross Kelly) and the Charles Ilfeld Company constructed warehouses near the tracks and began to flourish. A bank and the Las Vegas Normal School were built. The area around the yards continued to grow. The older Las Vegas across the Gallinas River refused to accept the upstart community, and referred to its neighbor as "New Town," and later, "East Las Vegas." Resentment flourished. The rest of the state began to take notice of the Las Vegas area and to think of it as the Denver of New Mexico—there seemed to be no limit to its prosperity.

By the time we arrived in August of 1931, Las Vegas was a booming area. The roundhouse was in operation, and the mercantile houses were bustling. Of particular interest to the trapping business was Joe Taichert's Fur and Hide Company, which was the largest in the southwest. Being the busy center of activity for the northeastern counties, small wonder Las Vegas was chosen as the headquarters for the game department's regional headquarters.

During our stay we found the townspeople of Las Vegas and the ranchers over the entire area to be extremely friendly and helpful. It was in those days that I first met ranchers W. O. Culberson, Alvin Stockton, John Morrow, and Ed Springer. Not only then, but in years to come, these men gave me their ardent support in my tasks and in my tribulations.

On about May 15,, 1932, five or so days before trout season began, I was trapping on horseback near the head of the Sapello Creek, near where Elliott Barker was raised. Through the bushes, I saw someone fishing in the creek. As I watched, he caught a fish, but he was so engrossed that he failed to see or hear me, although my horse was kicking rocks and making a lot of noise. When I was only fifteen to twenty yards away, he finally noticed me and made a dash for the weeds and thick brush, where he laid down and attempted to hide. I rode over to him and as he looked up sheepishly I smiled and, trying to be pleasant, asked him what kind of luck he was having.

EARLY DAYS IN THE GAME AND FISH DEPARTMENT

He had tried to remove the hook from the fish but had been unsuccessful, so I asked him not to throw it back. He was wearing overalls and had five more fish in his pockets, which he handed to me reluctantly for evidence. He then gave me his name and address and agreed to meet me at the office of the Justice of the Peace in Las Vegas the next day. This was the first case that I presented before a Justice of the Peace, so I asked my good friend, Mack Bruhl, U. S. Forest Ranger, to join me. In court, Charlie Higgens pleaded guilty and was fined twenty-five dollars. A short time later, Charlie Higgens, city attorney for Las Vegas, either resigned voluntarily or was asked to resign because he had broken the law.

By 1933, sportsmen and ranchers statewide were registering a considerable number of complaints with the Game Department concerning the damage to game and livestock by mountain lions. The New Mexico Game Commission, under the chairmanship of Colin Neblett, federal district judge, decided that a special and determined effort should be made to control the lions and reduce the damage. The Commission authorized the purchase of two trained lion dogs from the Lee brothers in Paradise, Arizona. I was chosen as lion hunter and at the same time was reassigned to Santa Fé, which would be my new headquarters. The dogs purchased were Crook and Buck, two invaluable helpers in the next few years. Crook, although purchased from the Lee brothers, was from Dub Evans' breed of hounds from the Beaverhead. With the dogs and my new responsibilities I would now cover the entire state.

At the time I received my new assignment, it was estimated that the mountain lion population in New Mexico was over 300. An adult lion can, and often will, kill one deer per week. Of the 300 lions, if only two-thirds were adults, the annual deer kill could be in the neighborhood of 10,000. Unfortunately, the lions would not ignore livestock, and whatever part of the enormous kill that was not deer, was, for the most part, livestock. The lions were scattered throughout the state and my task would not be easy. I would have to check each complaint within the boundaries of what was then the fifth largest state in the union, with over 93 million acres.

The U. S. Forest Service was one of the first to offer assistance to ranchers who reported lion attacks on their livestock. Forest supervisors and rangers offered me the use of ranger cabins, which were conveniently located throughout the state and were handy for me to use as shelter and as bases for hunting.

Once, during my first winter on my new job, I was camped at the Gallina Ranger Station, west of Coyote, where Albert and I had visited six years before. With me was Joe Rodriquez, U. S. forest ranger for the Coyote District. Because the Gallina station was used only as a temporary work cabin, Joe had permitted Mr. and Mrs. Neal Miller, formerly from Kansas City, to live and care for the house while Neal recuperated from tuberculosis. His wife, Ida, was a registered nurse and a marvelous cook.

Joe and I had been riding horseback in the deep snow north of Gallina looking for a herd of wild horses that were overgrazing the mesa area. The forest service was trying to reduce the wild herd because their numbers had increased until there was little grass left for cattle. At the north end of the mesa my dogs had found the tracks of three mountain lions, and had trailed them to where they had killed a deer in the deep snow. From the site of the kill it was a short race of only a few minutes until the dogs treed the lions. After the kill we skinned the lions and continued our search for the horses for the remainder of the day.

That evening after we had returned to the ranger station, and as we were recounting the events of the lion hunting to the Millers, Ida had an idea. She proposed that for dinner the next evening she would serve lion steaks, cooked according to her special recipe. She was so excited about the prospect that Joe and I promised to bring her a hind quarter from one of the yearling lions. When we found the carcass the next day, it was frozen solid, and we had a hard time removing the quarter. The meat was beautiful and resembled fresh pork or domestic rabbit. That evening, Neal carved the steaks and Ida began her

Santa Fe Railway Alvarado station, built in 1902 and torn down in 1970. Many New Mexicans have fond memories of the building. I stepped off the train April, 1927, and viewed this beautiful building enroute to northern New Mexico to begin a new life. (Santa Fe Railway photo)

Homer Pickens and his famous horse "Skip" waiting for Governor Jack Dempsey and Ranger Bruhl for a mountain lion hunt in the Gallina Canyon area above Las Vegas.

Homer and "Yankee Dan"—a young lion dog I was training in 1933.

My first mountain lion taken on Blue Bird Mesa, 1927, east of Cuba, N.M.

Hopewell mining town as it was in 1927 when we camped there while trapping wolves for the U.S. Biological Survey.

Wolf trapping camp in the Brazos country of Homer and Albert Pickens in 1927 east of Chama, New Mexico. Pictured: Homer-standing, Jess Hawley-sitting.

My lion hunting dogs "Crook", "Buck" and "Traylor" . . . saddle horse in background, 1932.

J. Stokley Ligon setting wolf trap near Beaverhead, New Mexico in 1922.

Homer trout fishing in Lagunitas Lakes on Carson National Forest in 1927 while trapping for wolves in the Brazos country.

Wild Turkey—In 1910 the wild turkey season was November 1st to December 31st, limit 4 per season. Trapping and transplanting by Dr. J. Stokley Ligon and I in 1937 from the Geo. Schiele ranch began to improve the turkey population in a new habitat across New Mexico on many interested ranches where they were protected.

Albert Pickens and lion dog "Sam" with Mr. Ben Lilly and his trail dog sitting on a pine log near the GOS Ranch north of Silver City, New Mexico. They were employed by the U.S. Biological Survey trapping wolves and hunting lions, 1922.

The first elk ever planted in the northern part of the state were put on the Urraca Ranch and Vermejo Park in 1911, by the Game Department. These elk were planted in the Jemez Mountains by the New Mexico Department of Game & Fish in 1947— Elk from Yellowstone National Park.

My rodent control crew working on Vermejo Park in 1930.

Homer Pickens cutting and storing ice at Seven Springs Fish Hatchery in 1937 for summer fish hauling and planting. W. B. Bletcher forman.

Packing into Gila Wilderness Area with U.S. Regional Forester Fred Kennedy, Ex-Governor John Simms, Senator Clinton P. Anderson, Sherburn Anderson, Ben Lemond Roberts and John Gatlin in 1956.

Mountain sheep released in Sandia Mountains in 1940 from Banff, Canada.

Deer are plentiful in most areas of the state due to the cooperation of conservation-minded ranchers and farmers, but coyote, bobcat and mountain lion still take their toll that the hunter should enjoy seeing and hunting.

Game Poacher Cabin, head of Pecos River, Santa Barber divide. Two illegal elk killed by poachers were found by U.S. Forest Ranger John Johnson and Homer Pickens and Bert Baca.

This mountain lion treed in Frijoles Canyon in 1932 before it was established as a U.S. National Park. Photo by Homer Pickens.

Dr. Edwin J. Smith treating the burned feet of little Smokey Bear at Santa Fe in 1950.

Homer C. Pickens and little Smokey Bear pose by Piper Cub plane before take off from Santa Fe, New Mexico for Washington, D.C., in June, 1950.

Homer posting trail signs on the Los Alamos forest area.

Tagging and monitoring the movement of young deer in the Los Alamos area.

Stockyard shipping corrals in Chama, New Mexico, built by Denver-Rio Grande Railway where Albert Pickens and I camped in 1927.

The antelope, once numerous all through the West, disappeared very rapidly upon encroachment by homesteaders in the early 1900's. About 1,700 antelope were estimated to be in New Mexico in 1910. 1937 trapping and transplanting of antelope was begun by the State Game Department, Paul Russell in charge, near San Augustine plains west of Magdalena on Montoso Ranch.

Mountain lion treed on a log by two good dogs, "Spot" and "Traylor", in the Jemez Mountains near Cuba, N.M., on Bluebird Mesa. Lion or cougar are common in the rough country where deer are plentiful.

Homer Pickens assisting Scouts in planting pine seedlings on burnover areas near Los Alamos.

Dr. L. M. Hollond checking trapped deer for experimental purposes. Los Alamos, 1966. Note telemetry on neck of deer.

Milton Bailey and Dr. Don Peterson tranqualizing a Los Alamos bear for a radio collar study while Jim Elmore looks on.

Horman Roser, Manager of Las Alamos AEC office in 1968, presenting the retirement certificate to Homer Pickens.

Badges and years of service stars with the N.M. Game & Fish Department, service on Los Alamos County Fair Board, member Kiwanis Club, Los Alamos.

Wild cow traps constructed in rugged Gila Wilderness Area in 1930. Used by the 916 Ranch to capture wild cattle.

First TAT commercial plane wreck in New Mexico in September, 1929. Photo by me while hunting lions on Mount Taylor, northeast of Grants, New Mexico.

Hunting lions while camped at Pine Springs Ranger Station, north of Los Alamos, 1933.

My pack outfit for rough country work.

Bobcat kitten, Jemez Mountain area, 1960.

Young mountain lion, Gila Wilderness Area, 1935.

Game Department personnel trapping and transplanting elk from Boy Scout ranch, Cimarron, New Mexico, 1938.

task. She cooked the steaks to a golden brown, chicken-fried style, and served them with hot biscuits and cream gravy. For two tired hunters after a weary winter day, it had all the appearance of being a meal fit for a king. The aroma of the food was appetizing, and I watched the others at the table as they began eating. There was much discourse on how delicious they found the meat to be. As I continued to watch, I recalled that Ben Lilly and my brother Albert had also said that lion meat was indeed tasty. In spite of all these fine recommendations, I found it difficult to take the first bite. I finally managed, but that first bite was also my last. For the rest of the meal I ate only biscuits and gravy. I am still not sure why. Perhaps it was the thought of handling and skinning so many lions and not the flavor of the meat that affected my appetite. Graciously Ida said that she understood my relunctance. I never again attempted to eat lion meat.

My friendship with Joe Rodriquez provided me with another memorable experience. Earlier in 1927, when I was with Albert, and we had camped by the Chama River near the historic town of Abiquiu, I first learned of Los Hermanos de Penitente, the brothers of penitents. This ancient secret religious offshoot of the Catholic Church had persisted in the southwest for centuries. Participants in the ceremonies seek to experience and to identify with Christ and the suffering that He endured during His journey to Mount Calvary and His crucifixion. Generally, very few outsiders are permitted to witness any part of the ceremonies, but even fewer are allowed to watch the journey to the Mount, which is a hill or high point in the area. Not by design, but by accident, Albert and I were camped near the Abiquiu Bridge and witnessed the procession of the cross. At daybreak, we were awakened in our camp by a strange chanting some distance from us. Curious, we arose and observed what appeared to be a hooded man struggling to carry a large wooden cross up a small hill west of the river. Following were several people singing. We strained to understand the words but could not. We made no attempt to move closer. They set the cross upright, and, after more chanting, which lasted for some time, the participants left the hill and marched to a small building nearby, where they disappeared. I learned later that the building with a small cross on top is called a Morada and serves as a meeting place for the Penitentes.

In April of 1934, Joe Rodriquez called me to meet him at his mother's home in the little village of Coyote to spend the night so we could rise early and witness the Penitente procession. I accepted, and in the twilight of the morning following my arrival, we climbed onto the roof and waited. At daylight, about a dozen people approached, chanting. We could clearly see a young man struggling with a large wooden cross and bleeding from his shoulders and back. Another man was dragging a horse skull bleached stark white. Two other men caught my eye as they vigorously whipped their own backs with what appeared to be rawhide straps, which they flung over their shoulders. They were dressed only in white shorts, and as they marched, their mournful chanting seemed to reflect their pain. We watched until they disappeared into the Morada.

That night Joe and I attended the services in the Morada. We sat on a long, plain wooden bench near the back row to the right of the center aisle. The room was dark except for light from candles on a cross atop the altar. Behind us and along each side I could hear strange noises that first startled me and then made my skin creep. There were rasping sounds that I never did identify, but I did recognize the sound of chains rattling. As the sounds increased in intensity, a man was brought before the cross for some special service which I could not understand and dared not at that moment ask Joe about. The noises ceased during the services but grew louder after the man was removed. Joe and I remained for about an hour and although I was bursting with curiosity afterwards, Joe offered no explanation, saying only that the participants had been reluctant to permit me to be present at all, and that it was best that we had left the Morada when we did so they could carry on the remainder of the services. I was aware, by 1934, that it was unusual for outsiders to witness the activities

EARLY DAYS IN THE GAME AND FISH DEPARTMENT

by any means, but as the years passed, I learned to appreciate fully just how unusual had been my experience in being permitted to enter a Morada and observe even a part of the ceremonies.

While I was lion hunting in the Jemez Mountains area the Seven Springs Fish Hatchery was under construction and there were as yet only a few ponds there. During a brief winter respite from lion hunting, I assisted W. B. Bletcher, who operated the hatchery, in storing ice to be used the next summer to cool the water in the old tank-type hatchery trucks. It was backbreaking work. We had to saw the ice from the fish pond and then store it in sawdust in the old building at the hatchery.

But we never looked at a timepiece. If there was a job to do, we did it, no matter what time of the day or night, and no one ever complained.

CHAPTER 9

LION HUNTING

AFTER WE ARRIVED in Santa Fé I found that the department was beseiged with reports of mountain lion damage. One of the pressing reports came from "Uncle" Benny Hyde, who said that a mountain lion was wreaking havoc on the deer population in the mountains above Santa Fé. According to his statement, the damage was heavy and the number of deer there was alarmingly low. He wanted the killing stopped. Uncle Benny was a noted orinthologist who lived in a mountain cabin, where he spent his time taking notes on birds in an area which would later bear his name. The first ski area for Santa Fé was Hyde Park, which still serves as a mountain playground and picnic area.

Mr. Barker asked me to checkout Uncle Benny's report. At that time, the route to Uncle Benny's cabin was much more difficult than it would be in a few more years. I was keeping my horse at the ranger station in Santa Fé Canyon. The station was in the area which is now between the two upper reservoirs that provide a water supply for Santa Fé. I saddled my horse, took the dogs and headed for Uncle Benny's cabin, all the while checking for lion sign. I came upon an isolated cabin that belonged to Thomas Benton Catron, an attorney, who as I later learned was one of the most famous and controversial politicians in New Mexico history. He was one of the two United States senators first elected when New Mexico was admitted to the Union in 1912. Hardly a book has been written about politics or famous trials in New Mexico that has failed to mention his name. He figured prominently in the Lincoln County War and was an attorney for the prosecution in the trial of Oliver Lee, who was accused and acquitted in a case involving the disappearance of Albert Jennings Fountain, a mystery which has never been solved. Senator Catron owned vast tracts of land, and it has been written that at one time he owned more combined acreage than anyone else in the history of the west.

The cabin that I came upon was located on a tract of possibly eighty acres, accessible only by wagon or horseback. As I approached the cabin, Senator Catron appeared and (suspiciously) confronted me. He was deaf, and my attempts to introduce myself were fruitless. He interrupted me abruptly and sternly ordered me off his property. I continued in my attempt to explain that I was on official business by telling him that I worked for Federal Judge Colin Neblett (chairman of the game commission), who was my highest supervisor, but the senator could not or possibly would not hear me. Rebuked and angered, I returned to the ranger station, where I left my horse and, in my Model A, went back to Santa Fé. The next morning, I informed Mr. Barker of what occurred, and he advised me to see Judge Neblett, which I did. Judge Neblett was in his office at the federal court house, and he invited me in immediately. I repeated my story, and in his distinctive southern drawl he said, "You leave it to me, Homah. I'll take care of it and don't you hesitate any more to do your duty. You go anywhea you want to go up theah whether you are on ole Tom Catron's property or not."

The next time I saw Senator Catron, I could hardly believe he was the same person. Obviously Judge Neblett had discussed the matter with him, true to his word. I was invited into his cabin for coffee and from that day forward we were friends and I was always welcome.

In August of 1932 I had a second close encounter with a mountain lion while once again hunting in the Jemez Mountains. One could almost infer that lions in these mountains were more dangerous than elsewhere, but this is not really the case. It is just that I seemed to have a talent for getting myself into trouble in that area.

LION HUNTING

On this occasion, I was camped in Water Canyon, south of the Los Alamos Ranch School in an area now known as the "S" site project. While I was hunting, my dogs had treed a lion on the mesa between Frijole and Alamo canyons. The lion was in a large pine tree perhaps seventy-five to ninety feet tall. The first limb was about fifty feet from the ground. At that time I was still using a .32-.20 Colt revolver, a Bisley model. I took a shot at the lion with the pistol and only slightly wounded the animal in the hind leg or hip. The lion was almost grown and weighed about ninety pounds. It bolted down from the tree, but because the ground was level and the dogs' line of sight was excellent, they were able to watch its every move. When it hit the ground, the dogs, five of them, always unafraid, tied into the lion and began to give it quite a beating —at first. As the lion bit one dog the other dogs attacked it from the rear. It would turn one dog loose and then grab or claw another. Gradually, the lion really began to hurt the dogs. Before I knew it I was in the thick of the battle myself. The dogs were all around me and the lion could not get away. I had to do something—not only for the dogs, but also for myself. I could not shoot the lion for fear of hitting one of my dogs, so I decided my only hope was to move in and try to hit the lion in the head with my heavy six-shooter. I was almost in position to strike the cat when it bit one of the dogs and then let it loose. The dog nearest to me bit the lion on the rear and the cat wheeled to get that dog. As I turned, I raised my arm to strike the blow and the lion caught my movement. It poised to grab me instead of the dog, and I jumped backwards to avoid the claws. I was wearing heavy chaps, which made it awkward for me to move easily, and to compound the problem, when I jumped backwards my spur caught on a small pine log. I unceremoniously fell flat on my rear. As I went down, it occured to me that my time had come, because that lion had me—and I knew it. But before the lion could pounce, another dog grabbed it on the rear and it turned, giving me time to get up. On my feet, I realized that I still could not shoot, so I decided to try again to strike the lion. I worked my way back into the melee and this time succeeded in hitting the lion with my pistol, which allowed the dogs to finish it.

On another occasion, I was lion hunting in the Jemez Mountains east of Cuba, operating from the Bluebird Ranch, which was owned by Richard Wetherill, the assistant forest ranger. I covered the San Pablo Canyon, Señorita Canyon, and Red Top Lookout Mountain areas. Dick was usually busy doing other things, but we rode together some. One morning I left early and headed east, the shortest way to the top of Bluebird Mesa. I ran into a mountain lion track and the dogs trailed it into San Pablo Canyon and up to the south end of Bluebird Mesa under the rim, where we found the lion and the dogs treed it. The canyon where the lion was treed, a tributary of San Pablo Canyon, is small and narrow, with rimrock forming high cliffs on both sides. All the dogs but one were barking at the base of the cliff. The remaining dog was on top of the cliff, which was about a hundred feet high. In order to see the lion, I had to get around to the head of the canyon. When I reached a vantage point, I could see the top of the lion's head in a crack in the rock about halfway down from the top of the cliff. He was so well concealed that I could not get a shot, but taking lions was my job, so I decided to see if I could somehow get closer. I tied my horse and climbed down the cliff, using the same route that the dogs had used. When I was still about 200 feet from the lion, I found where the lion had entered the crack in the rock, which was about 50 feet from the bottom of the cliff. There was a tiny ledge just wide enough for the lion, but for some reason the dogs would not use the ledge and would not enter. I surveyed the ledge and decided I could get through. My Model 94 .30-.30 Winchester was ideal for this situation. I had cut off the barrel to fifteen inches, so I could easily pack it in my saddle and not worry about hanging it in brush. I got down on my hands and knees and slowly crawled in, hanging onto anything I could occasionally dragging the rifle. I finally reached a split in the rock that widened above me. In the space back in the split was the lion. I could not get up to the split easily because a wedge of rock stuck out and would force me to climb up to see or get a shot. I knew that when I did get up over the jutting wedge I would probably be face-to-face with the lion, but I decided to chance it. My rifle was loaded. I had it in my right hand, but I had to use both hands to climb. So I placed the rifle on the rock, cupped my hand over it, and slowly pulled myself upwards. My worst fears were suddenly realized. When I pulled myself up, the lion was about three feet from my face. I could not turn loose with either hand and obviously could not aim or fire the rifle. I was in a bad spot, and there was nothing I could do but stare at the lion. There was no other way out for the lion either. It crouched, and then almost before I had a chance to duck, it leaped over my head and landed on the ledge behind me. I still could do nothing as the lion raced off. I let myself down, turned around, slowly crawled back the way I had entered, and made it back to my horse. The dogs had spotted the lion, chased it off the rim on the west side toward the house at Bluebird Ranch, and again treed it in dense timber. As I rode along I was still nervous and upset. I had taken a dangerous chance and although I had escaped unscathed I promised myself I would never climb in under such conditions again. I realized it had been a fool move, especially since I was alone. As I approached the lion again, he jumped from the tree and ran down the slope and leaped into a large yellow pine surrounded by thick oak brush. I rode around the tree to a level area and tied my horse in a spot where I could shoot the lion and avoid giving him the opportunity to jump from the tree and run again. Thinking back on the incident, I would have to say that my experience on that ledge was probably the most dangerous thing I ever attempted during my four years of lion hunting for the game and fish department.

During 1932 I killed thirty-six mountain lions in the Jemez Mountains, ten of which I took from above the area that would one day be Bandelier National Mounment.

CHAPTER 10

FRANK HIBBEN

IN THE LATE summer of 1934, just before I was transferred from Santa Fé to Silver City, I camped in Water Canyon, on the east side of a wagon road (now New Mexico 4) from Ted Mathers' log house. Mathers was the caretaker for the horses at the Los Alamos Ranch School. At that campsite I ate bear meat for the first time. Mr. and Mrs. Ted Mathers invited me to have breakfast with them one morning. Ted had recently killed a small bear for their winter meat supply, and when I crossed the road to eat with them they served hot biscuits, gravy, eggs and nice big slices of ham from the bear's hind quarter. The meat, as I remember, tasted very much like ham. It was a delicious breakfast.

A short time later I was notified by Elliott Barker that the Southwest Conservation League, directed by himself, Judge C. M. Botts, and Arthur Pack, had employed Frank Hibben to study the habits of mountain lions in New Mexico and Arizona. Hibben arrived at my camp in Water Canyon in a Model A Ford truck pulling his horse in a trailer. The horse was a flea-bitten gray that he had bought from the Navahos. He had previously been employed as caretaker of Ghost Ranch, whose owner, Arthur Peck, was providing funds for the lion study. When Hibben, who was a graduate of Princeton and Harvard, introduced himself to me, my first impression was that he was an eastern dude. But after he set up camp with me and we began swapping stories, I changed my mind.

As we sat around the campfire, Frank explained to me how he was going to conduct his study and what role I was going to play in it. He was going to accompany me on the hunt and collect scat (droppings) and stomach contents, which would be sent to the biology lab at the University of New Mexico to be analyzed by Drs. E. F. Castetter and John D. Clark. When we were on the trail, Frank carried a bag to collect scat, and a pad on which to note locations, weather conditions, altitude, and anything else relevant to the habits of mountain lions.

Several weeks after we began working together, Frank left to study lions in Arizona with U. S. Biological Survey hunters there, and I was transferred to Silver City. But in the course of his study, which continued through September of 1935, Frank often joined me on hunts around Silver City. We, my dogs, and the Navaho horse had good times together, although on one occasion we had to lay out on the trail with no tent and no food. Once, near the confluence of the East Fork and the West Fork of the Gila River, we came upon the camp of two prospectors who had packed into the area with burros. I found that they had killed a deer illegally and took them both to Silver City to be prosecuted.

Once Frank captured two lion cubs while on a hunt in Arizona. He brought them back to his motor hotel, where he left them for awhile to attend other business. When he returned, he found a real mess. The cubs had ripped the drapes to shreds and had turned on the bathtub faucet, flooding the whole room. Frank had to pay all the damages!

Frank and I became lifelong friends, and he always enjoyed stretching the truth a little about our exploits when he told about them. He was a good camp cook and enjoyed cutting off mountain lion steaks and cooking them in the dutch oven. I enjoyed his enthusiasm but never ate his lion steaks.

Frank published the results of his study in an article entitled "A Preliminary Study of the Mountain Lion *Felis oregonensis*," which appeared in *The University of New Mexico Bulletin* in 1937.

CHAPTER 11

JUST DOING MY JOB

IN THE LATE summer of 1936, I was transferred from Silver City to Albuquerque. By that time I had killed or captured 160 mountain lions—more than anyone else on official record. Many of the lions I had captured were sent to zoos: two young ones went to the Smithsonian Zoo in Washington, two to the Clovis zoo, and two to the zoo in Albuquerque.

When I was transferred to Albuquerque, the city had a population of between forty and fifty thousand people. Because I was doing public relations work for the New Mexico Game and Fish Department, I soon became acquainted with many of the business people in town and the farmers and ranchers in the valley. I continued to keep a couple of lion dogs and to do a little lion hunting when I could get away from my other work. I took a total of seven mountain lions in the Sandias. I was then patrolling from Albuquerque to the northwest corner of the state, including the area bounded by Mountainair, Santa Fé, Chama, Aztec, Farmington, Gallup, and Belen. One of the more interesting incidents of my Albuquerque duty occured when I prosecuted several TWA pilots. On their layover time in Albuquerque these men flew their private plane up and down the Rio Grande river hunting ducks and quail. But although they only laid over in Albuquerque, they bought resident instead of nonresident licenses. Among those prosecuted were Jack Fry, recently president of TWA, and Otis Bryan, who later flew President Franklin Delano Roosevelt to Tehran for his conference with Joseph Stalin and Winston Churchill. Bryan later became a neighbor in Albuquerque. Magistrate

Judge E. C. Gober and Justice of the Peace Leonard Tartaglia heard the cases.

While I was located in Albuquerque I was only one of five district wardens, who were then under State Game Warden Elliott Barker. Warden Barker did not have an assistant, but he did have an office assistant and two secretaries. All worked in one room in the old capitol building in Santa Fé.

The New Mexico Game and Fish Department then maintained the Seven Springs Fish Hatchery, which it had just begun to improve, as well as the Lisboa Springs Hatchery on the Pecos, and the Jenks Cabin Hatchery at the junction of the White Creek and West Fork of the Gila River. This last hatchery was remote, and men and materials had to be packed in. It was later sold to the U.S. Forest Service, and the department developed a hatchery at Glenwood, on the west side of the Mogollon Mountains. This was a very small operation—mainly a rearing pond. When I was first employed by the department there was a small hatchery just below the town of Chama, but this was not a paying proposition and was finally sold. The department then bought the Parkview site and developed a satisfactory and profitable hatchery that is still in operation.

Occasionally I worked at the Seven Springs Hatchery with the foreman, W. B. Bletcher, and his one assistant. I carried lots of fish around, transferring them from tank to tank in ten-gallon milk cans.

Before the C.C.C. (Civilian Conservation Corps) built a road into what is now Bandelier National Monument, the small hotel in Frijoles Canyon operated by George Fry and his wife could only be reached by saddle mule. The hotel got many of its supplies by way of a small tram run by a gasoline motor. That tram was the logical way to bring the fish into the canyon, and that was how we did it! When the fish reached the bottom, George Fry and I put them in his wagon, and he drove the team up and down the river while I released the trout.

In May of 1937 I received a call from the state police asking me to assist in a search for three school teachers who had become lost in a vast wild area south of Grants. The teachers, tourists from Tennessee, had driven down to visit the ice caves. The women were totally unaccustomed to the land and knew nothing of the problems of traveling in semiarid country. They had parked their car, and while inspecting the ice caves had become disoriented. They had wandered away from their car and were unable to locate it.

When the word went out that the teachers had not returned to their lodgings, it was not long before Clyde Tingley, then governor, mobilized the state police and anyone else he could think of, including a large group of men who were working in a C.C.C. camp in Grants.

When I arrived in the area with a saddle horse and one lion dog, I set out immediately to search for tracks or any sign that the women might have left. After a while, my dog and I reached the lava flow called by the Spanish malpais ("bad foot") because of its rough, grotesque surface that has been fractured by cooling and distorted by collapse. The surface can tear a person's shoes or feet to shreds; hence the descriptive name for it.

The malpais was too rough for my horse, so my dog and I had to continue without him. My dog was eager to help, and with his assistance I found twigs and limbs broken here and there—all leading farther into the malpais. A foreboding feeling came over me when I found a woman's shoe. Several yards beyond, I found another. This was no place to be without shoes. Five days had passed since the teachers had begun their wanderings, and each man in the field knew that we would soon run out of time—if we had not already.

I had taken a small lunch on the hunt—a sandwich and an orange—which I carried inside my shirt. Late in the afternoon I sat down on one of the large lava rocks and ate the sandwich. I had just taken the orange out of my shirt when I suddenly spied one of the women in the distance, apparently sitting but not moving.

When I reached her, she slowly opened her eyes and stared at me blankly, not comprehending that someone had found her. She was totally exhausted and obviously dehydrated. I offered her a drink from my canteen and had to restrain her from gulping the water. I cut the orange and offered her a slice. She literallly snatched it from my hand. Before she could finish it, she fainted. In a moment she recovered and regained her wits, calmed down, and quietly ate the orange.

I fired a shot from my revolver to summon the C.C.C. men in my area. When they arrived they assembled a stretcher and carried her out to a waiting ambulance.

After I had found the first teacher we had a good fix on the area we needed to search. The C.C.C. men shortly found the other two women, who were alive but in poor shape. Both had lost control of their senses, and we were worried that they might not pull through, but in the end all three teachers recovered from the ordeal—a happy ending to what could have easily become a tragedy. The ice caves are located forty miles southwest of Grants, New Mexico, and are an important tourist attraction for people traveling Interstate 40.

CHAPTER **12**

TRAPPING AND TRANSPLANTING GAME AND BIRDS

IN THE FALL of 1937 J. Stokley Ligon and I trapped turkeys above Mora on the Hall's Peak Game Refuge and on the Schelie Ranch. The days were cold and snowy, and we heated rocks in the campfire at night to keep our feet warm the next day.

Ligon, author of the well-known *Birds of New Mexico,* was a pioneer ornithologist in New Mexico and was perhaps more knowledgeable about the birds of the southwest than any other person. Owner of the first game bird farm in New Mexico, he had developed many different kinds of bird traps used by the U.S. Biological Survey, for which he was the district agent from 1915 to 1921.

We used some traps of Ligon's design to catch the turkeys for transplanting. The log traps were about four feet high, ten feet wide, and twenty feet long. There were doors three feet square on either end of the traps, and when turkeys wandered into the trap, we released a pin that dropped netting down over both entrances. The logs that made the trap were spaced for light and ventilation, and the top of the traps were thatched with hay to protect the birds from weather and make the traps dark.

When we had captured twelve turkeys—a full load for two pickups—we transplanted them to both an area north of Aztec and to the Animas Mountains south of Lordsburg. We tried to release two hens and one tom at each suitable place we stopped in the transplanting areas.

TRAPPING AND TRANSPLANTING GAME AND BIRDS

In the spring of 1938 the New Mexico Game and Fish Department received a shipment of elk from Oklahoma in exchange for some antelope that we had trapped on the San Augustin Plains and sent to the Washita Mountains Game Refuge near Lawton, Oklahoma. The elk were delivered to an area east of the village of San Mateo on Floyd Lee's stock grazing range near Mount Taylor—an excellent elk country. In fact, elk were once plentiful in the beautiful forests of Mount Taylor, but the animals were exterminated in the late 1800's, and there had been none since that time. This was the first attempt to renew the herds, and it proved to be a sound move.

Six elk were delivered in two trucks, each animal in a separate crate. The herd gradually increased over the years until finally the department was able to allow bull elk hunting throughout the Mount Taylor area.

On the day that we released the elk, the school at San Mateo dismissed the children so they could see the first elk ever to be released in the area. The teachers and children arrived in a station wagon, and it was an exciting event for them. The department had permission from Floyd Lee and from the forest service to make the release.

Sometime later I received a call from a Mr. Bibo in Ceboyeta, on the east side of Mount Taylor, stating that the townsfolk had a problem with a bull elk. The bull had wandered into the area and was eating fresh corn when it was discovered and herded into an old adobe house, where they had confined it. This was in the summer, when the corn was four or five feet tall. The bull had damaged quite a bit of the corn, but the people had no desire to harm him. In fact, they were somewhat taken with him, because for some reason he seemed to be partially tame. When I arrived, I saddled my horse, and then we released the bull. I rode up to him and fired several shots into the air; the bull, startled, ran for what he must have thought was his life. I chased him on horseback until I ran him quite a distance from Ceboyeta. I have no idea whatever happened to that elk, but because he was partially tame, he may have landed on someone's table long before the first hunting season ever began. At any rate, he never went back to eat fresh corn at Ceboyeta.

In 1939 I was again assigned to accompany J. Stokely Ligon, this time to Wyoming to trap sage chickens in an attempt to restock the area between Taos and Tres Piedras along the rim of the Rio Grande canyon—all sage country. At one time, sage chickens were native in that area, but they had been severely depleted by hunters years before.

We also trapped Barbary sheep near Roswell. The sheep originally came from the Atlas Mountains in northwest Africa, and some ranchers, Joe McKnight in the Roswell country for example, bought some of them. They flourished and soon became overstocked. We trapped some of these sheep and transplanted them to the Canadian River country and to the northwest corner of the state. The department also purchased some Barbary sheep from the Hearst Game Farm near San Diego, California, and we released them in the Canadian River area and in the rough country east of Aztec, New Mexico.

Late in 1939—winter had already arrived—the department received three shipments of Rocky Mountain Bighorn sheep from Bath, Canada. They came three per shipment. I released these animals in Pino Canyon in the Sandia Mountains east of Albuquerque with the assistance of Fred Arthur, U. S. Forest Service supervisor and Louis H. Laney of the U.S. Fish and Wildlife Service. Two more releases were subsequently made, one in 1940 and one in 1941. That was the start of the Rocky Mountain Bighorn sheep herd in the Sandias, although these mountains were recorded as a habitat for the sheep back in the late 1890s.

In 1940, the New Mexico Game Commission decided the department had grown to the point that Elliott Barker needed an assistant. I was chosen as assistant director and was transferred once again to Santa Fé, where I served in that capacity until 1953, when Elliott retired. During that time, I was a dedicated employee of the department. I loved my work, and because of that I tried hard to carry out all of Mr. Barker's wishes and to assist him in any way I could to improve the department and its relationship with the public.

TRAPPING AND TRANSPLANTING GAME AND BIRDS

By 1940, the department had grown a great deal. For the predatory animal control efforts were approximately twenty-five trappers and two lion hunters. In addition, some Work Projects Administration men, paid partly by the W.P.A. and partly by the New Mexico Game and Fish Department, were under the direction of the department. The men, distributed all over the state, worked under me. I traveled over the state directing their activity and coordinating their work with the needs of the public—mainly ranchers, farmers and forestry officials.

At the same time, I continued to work more generally in public relations—possibly one of my more important functions. This I enjoyed greatly because I have always liked people and enjoyed making new friends. My other work included special patrols, managing special hunts for mountain sheep, Barbary sheep, antelope, deer, and other big game.

I also assisted in some of the work at the fish hatcheries—especially in public relations. The department felt it was important to familiarize the general public with the work of the hatcheries. More new employees were being added all the time, including biologists to study game problems and fish specialists and engineers to improve our construction at the hatcheries and at small dams such as the Fenton Lake Dam on Cebolla Creek below the Seven Springs Fish Hatchery.

CHAPTER 13

LAW ENFORCEMENT

IN THE SPRING of 1941, I received a call from Speed Simmons, the department patrolman along the Pecos, telling me that he had received a report that someone had killed a deer above Cowles on forest land. Speed asked if I could join him in looking into the matter, so I drove to Cowles to join him.

Cowles was mainly a post office at that time, operated by George Viles, who also had a store and the Mountain View Lodge. In the main lodge was the head and hide of a grizzly bear that George, then a forest ranger, had killed about 1900 on the head of the Pecos River.

I got a saddle horse from George and rode with Speed in a northeasterly direction from the lodge toward Mora Creek and Mora Flats, where the Valdez and Mora creeks join. Before we reached the top, we saw where a pickup truck had backed around and driven over a gopher mound. The tread was easily identifiable and this clue was a big help later. We then found the intestines of a deer that had been killed on the spot. Judging from the location of the pickup we were able to ascertain the trajectory of the bullet that had killed the deer. We found the slug embedded near the base of an aspen tree. The tree was green, and we easily removed the slug. It had mushroomed some and still had blood and hair on it. We followed the tire tracks down the slope, and they led to Geronimo Gonzales' ranch house, which was a couple of miles northeast of the Mountain View Lodge.

We rode back to the Lodge and drove to the Justice of the Peace in Pecos, where we made out an affidavit stating that to the best of our knowledge there was an illegal deer concealed in the house. On the basis of this evidence we obtained a search warrant.

When we returned to Geronimo's there was no one at home. Again we left, but returned later in the day. This time Geronimo and his brother Magdaleno, who operated a bar at Terrero, were at home. We served the warrant and with their permission began searching the house. We found the rifle on the bed under a quilt. In an adjoining room we found the hind quarters of a freshly killed deer. Magdaleno admitted killing the deer, so we asked him to go with us to see Justice of Peace Rivera in the town of Pecos.

Before the judge, Magdaleno pleaded not guilty. The Judge fined him $50 and court costs. Magdaleno appealed the case to the district court in Las Vegas, San Miguel County, where the deer was killed. The district judge was Judge Armijo, now deceased. In court, Magdaleno was represented by an attorney, but with the evidence presented, Judge Armijo upheld the decision of the justice of the peace and fined Magdaleno $200 plus $50 court costs.

Still full of fight, Magdaleno appealed to the state supreme court, and lost. The supreme court ordered confiscation of the truck Magdaleno had used in commission of the offense. In all, his fruitless efforts cost him about $1,150, and he could have gotten off for $55 at first. Magdaleno was, about that time, an official in San Miguel County. I have always wondered why he pursued the matter as he did. But he had his reasons whatever they were. Magdaleno, Geronimo and I have, however, remained good friends throughout the years following the incident.

In October of 1945, I was directing an antelope hunt around Border Hill, near Tinnie, New Mexico, and the Diamond A Ranch west of Roswell. One morning during the hunt I had to leave at daylight to give a talk before the Game Protective Association meeting that evening in Albuquerque. On the highway west of Roswell I passed a car with Texas license plates moving slowly and suspiciously along the highway. As I went around the car I observed four men, one of whom had a rifle.

LAW ENFORCEMENT

I went over the next hill, traveling fast, and as soon as I was out of sight, I turned my car around and started back and passed them again going the other way. They were still moving slowly. Out of sight once more, I turned around and began following them back from a distance to see what would happen.

Topping the hill, I suddenly came upon the men just as one of them fired from the car and killed an antelope on the Diamond A Ranch just across the fence. Startled, I continued to watch. Two of the men jumped out, taking the rifle with them, and climbed over the fence to retrieve the antelope.

As they began dragging it back to the fence I drove up, my bumper to theirs, and began searching their car as the doors were open. I saw no other firearms but did see two butcher knives. When the two men saw me drive up and stop, they dropped the antelope and tried to hide the rifle before they began walking back to the fence. I identified myself, arrested the men and retrieved both the rifle and the antelope. I had the men drive ahead of me to the justice of the peace at the courthouse in Roswell. The justice of the peace quickly assessed a $100 fine on the man who had fired the rifle. He did not have that much money with him, so he was put in jail before he realized he could call home to Texas for the money, which he quickly did. The money was wired to him, and he was released after he paid his fine. Having finished my duties on the matter, I proceded to the meeting in Albuquerque that evening.

> *Santa Fe New Mexican,* August 4, 1946:
> "Assistant State Game Warden Homer Pickens said today that a group of 25 soldiers from Kirtland Field, Albuquerque, under the command of a lieutenant last Sunday stole dynamite caps from the U. S. Forest Service . . . and dynamited fish out of the Pecos River."

At the time, Elliott Barker was ill and confined in St. Vincent Hospital in Santa Fé, and I was acting state game warden, handling all affairs of the department. On August 3, we received a telephone call from a Spanish family living upstream from the Pecos Fish Hatchery and downstream of the Brush Ranch. The caller was Marcelino Gutierrez, who stated that he saw dead fish floating down the river a short distance below where a group of soldiers in a bus had spent a couple of days.

I immediately called Bert Baca, our district game warden, and told him to get rolling. By the time he arrived the bus had departed, but a lieutenant and four enlisted men were still there cleaning up the area. Bert, accompanied by another warden, L. W. "Speed" Simmons, arrested the five men and took them to jail in Las Vegas.

At that time, the Terrero mine, three or four miles upstream of the spot where the incident occurred, was abandoned. The mine portal was boarded up and the U. S. Forest Service was using it for the storage of dynamite and caps. Evidence indicated that the soldiers broke into the mine by prying the lock and removed some dynamite, 500 electric caps, and a detonator. They evidently carried the contraband to the second bridge below the mines, where, with the electric wire, they lined the river with blasting caps, which they placed one or two feet apart, and wired to the detonator. Undoubtedly, some of the men were experienced in handling explosives.

When they fired the caps, the detonator killed a large number of trout, and those they were unable to retrieve were spotted by Marcelino Gutierrez. Baca and Simmons also found a few dead trout.

Monday morning I called the commanding officer at Kirtland, explained the situation, and asked for the names and the return of the remaining soldiers involved. I explained also that the men would face charges of illegal possession of explosives and dynamiting waters of the Pecos River. That morning one of the soldiers had shipped out to Korea. The other nineteen men were returned, but the commanding officer at Kirtland asked me to explain the procedures and policies concerning the situation. He then asked me to drop the charges. He said that the lieutenant would lose his rank for permitting the incident to occur. I told him that the men would have to face the courts the same as any other citizen.

I then advised the justice of the peace in Pecos that we would have the group there that day. Bert Baca and I went to the West Las Vegas Court House to pick up the lieutenant and the four enlisted men. A wave of compassion came over me as I saw the men, who had slept in their uniforms that night. The lieutenant looked crestfallen, for he knew the consequences for burglarizing the mine and stealing government property.

The bus with the other men did not arrive until Tuesday and the men were delivered to the justice of the peace. The officer accompanying the men advised them to enter their pleas individually; the procedure therefore was very time consuming. Justice Rivera called out the amount of each fine as it was assessed individually. After the last assessment, the total of the fines for the entire group was given and the finance officer, who had brought cash, paid in full the amount for the entire process.

This incident involved more people than any I had been involved with before or since. Each man was fined $25 and $5 court costs, for a total assessment of $720. Considering that a fine of $300 was levied against another individual apprehended after dynamiting fish in the Rio Grande a few years later, the soldiers were fined rather lightly. I never heard what consequences they suffered for their theft of federal property, and I don't know what happened to the lieutenant.

CHAPTER 14

SMOKEY THE BEAR

IN MAY OF 1950 a large fire burned over 18,000 acres of the Lincoln National Forest in the Capitan Mountains west of Roswell, New Mexico. The fire not only destroyed valuable timber and ground cover, but also wiped out an inestimable amount of wildlife. One animal that survived the fire eventually became a nationally famous symbol and reminder of the terrible destruction that forest fires wreck on the plants and helpless wildlife of the forest. This fire was the beginning of the story of Smokey the Bear.

As the fire grew, every citizen and every agency, including the U. S. Army from Fort Bliss in El Paso, Texas, was called on to assist in fighting the huge blaze. Members of the New Mexico Game and Fish Department were there, too. Speed Simmons was in charge of a group of soldiers assigned to one side of Capitan Mountain when the fire crowned out and passed over them. They escaped being burned alive by flattening themselves among rocks, and covering their heads with handkerchief soaked with water from their canteens.

After the fire passed over, the men heard squealing nearby. Upon investigation, they discovered a tiny bear cub a few feet off the ground in a small oak tree. The little bear's chocolate brown fur was thoroughly singed, and its feet were badly burned. The pitiful sounds it made touched all the men. They searched the area thoroughly but found no trace of its mother or any other cubs. Speed removed the whimpering little animal from the tree and carried it to the fire camp.

Ray Bell, also from the department, put the bear in the department plane and flew it to Santa Fé, where Ray's wife Ruth and I met them. We took the animal to Dr. Ed Smith's veterinarian hospital, where it was treated for burns. The Bells and my family took care of the animal for several weeks as he recuperated and developed an onery disposition.

In the meantime, the U. S. Forest Service, with the encouragement of the Department, decided the bear could provide a great service to the nation if it were to become the living concept of the Forest Service's emblem for fire prevention, Smokey the Bear. The idea moved rapidly through the ranks and plans were made to present Smokey to the Boy and Girl Scouts of America. He would be flown to Washington, D. C., where, during dedication ceremonies, he would be given to the Rock Creek Zoological Garden. After negotiations between the department and the forest service, plans were completed. The news media between Santa Fé and Washington were contacted to give as much publicity as possible at the air terminals between the two cities. So far as everyone was concerned, the sooner the program was underway the better, because it was a hot, dry year and forest fires were a problem throughout the nation.

About the middle of June, Mr. Piper, maunfacturer of the Piper Cub airplane, was asked if he would provide a plane to fly Smokey to Washington. Frank Hines, a Piper Company agent who owned an airport in Hobbs, New Mexico, was chosen as the pilot. I was chosen to escort and take care of Smokey during the trip. After we constructed a small cage and I obtained a harness and a leash for Smokey, we were ready. Jim Young, a Santa Fé artist, painted on the fuselage of the brand new Piper Tri-pacer a picture of Smokey with his arm in a sling to emphasize Smokey's harrowing experience in the forest fire. Kay Flock, then supervisor of the Santa Fé National Forest, was assigned to fly with us to Cleveland, where he would deplane. So the three of us and Smokey, harnessed and secured in his cage, which resembled a wire suitcase, left Santa Fé.

Amarillo, Texas, was our first stop. There, and during succeeding stops in Tulsa, Kansas City, and St. Louis, where we spent the first night, people and the news media greeted us with friendly interest. In St. Louis we were met by a large black limousine that had been provided to take us to the Chase Manhattan Hotel.

The crowds grew larger at each successive stop. The second day, after Kay Flock left us in Cleveland, we flew on to Cincinnati, where we were treated to a grand reception and spent the second night. We were taken to Louisville, and we were also well received there. The third day we flew to Baltimore, where we had to wait before we were scheduled to land at the Washington airport. In Baltimore, Smokey was taken to a Veterinarian hospital for a routine check to make sure that he suffered no ill effects from the trip. On the last morning, we were greeted by a heavy rainstorm. It seemed that it would be almost impossible to make it into Washington, but Frank Hines was a good pilot and took us in without difficulty.

In Washington we were greeted with a large crowd and great fanfare. Senator Dennis Chavez and Homer Pickens, Jr., then working for the Federal Bureau of Investigation, were there to greet us. At the airport we were taken to the presidential press conference room by representatives of the Boy and Girl Scouts of America and by a large contingent of airline hostesses. Also there to meet us were Mr. Piper, Lyle Watts, the U. S. Forester, Lloyd Swift, chief of wildlife resources for the U. S. Forest Service, and Morgan Smith, public relations officer for the forest service. Arrangements were made for Smokey to be taken to the Rock Creek Zoological Garden in care of Dr. Mann, the director of the zoo.

The next day my son Homer, Norman Brown, Senator Dennis Chavez, and the distinguished gentlemen who had greeted us the previous day attended the ceremony in which Smokey was dedicated to the Boy and Girl Scouts, many of whom had come from nearby communities for the ceremonies.

From the beginning Smokey was the center of attention. He only weighed about ten pounds, but I had to wear my buckskin gloves at all times, because he had a tendency to bite when I least expected it. Everyone, children and grownups alike, wanted to touch or cuddle the little bear. My primary responsibility, I had thought, would be to protect Smokey. But as it turned out I found I more often had to protect his admirers.

Smokey never hesitated to go after anyone who came within reach of his tiny claws.

The crowd was huge, and there were many speakers. A movie I began in Santa Fé recorded the events of the trip and was completed with the dedication. William Boyd, better known as Hopalong Cassidy, narrated the last half of the color movie, which was subsequently made in many different languages and shown throughout the world in a global effort to popularize Smokey and carry the message that safe practices can do much to reduce the forest fire hazard. For his efforts, Hopalong was made an honorary forest ranger by Lyle Watts. In addition to the movie, a comic book that depicted the story of Smokey was designed and published under the direction of the forest service. Many slogans came out of the awareness that resulted from the publicity for the little bear, the most popular of which was: "Only you can prevent forest fires."

Smokey began to thrive in his new home in Washington. People from the world over came to view the living symbol of forest fire prevention. He grew to be a rather large bear, weighing 500 pounds. In 1962 the U. S. Department of Agriculture decided that it was time for Smokey to have an heir, so it sent in a tawny bear named Goldie to brighten Smokey's bachelorhood. But the two failed to produce any offspring.

In 1971, the agriculture department found another little bear, also orphaned, in the Lincoln National Forest—the same forest where Smokey was found twenty-one years before. The New Mexico Game and Fish Department had received reports that an undernourished and scrawny cub weighing about forty pounds had become a nuisance in the area by stealing food wherever he could. He was discovered wandering alone and homeless in the Cloudcroft district and taken to the Alamogordo zoo. Before he was taken to Washington, D. C., to become the official heir, he, unlike the original Smokey, had become playful and affectionate by the time he weighed about a hundred pounds.

In 1968, Edna and I purchased a travel trailer and were spending the summer traveling around the U. S. visiting and

SMOKEY THE BEAR

taking in the sights that we had never found the time to see before. Near the headwaters of the Salmon River in Stanley, Idaho, we stopped at the Stanley Lake Trailer Park Campground for the night. The young forest ranger and his wife came by and invited us to attend an outdoor program including movies that would be presented after dark. With nothing else to do, we drove over to the program area. The first movie shown was the story of Smokey the Bear, which of course included his rescue in the Capitan Mountains and my taking the little bear to Washington. After the show I introduced myself to the young ranger, who was startled to say the least. He lamented that if he had only known beforehand, he would have asked me to address the people before the movie was shown. Unfortunately, we were expected by friends and had to leave the next morning, but the look of surprise on the ranger's face I shall not soon forget.

The final chapter in the story of the original Smokey the Bear began on November 8, 1976, when he died. Smokey had lived far beyond the life expectancy of his kind. The black bear, *Ursus americanus,* generally lives ten to twelve years in the wild. Smokey was twenty-seven but had become feeble and gray and resembled a grizzly. The zoo keepers knew that his time was coming, and the word had gone out. It was decided that it would be only fitting that Smokey be returned to his native land in the mountains of New Mexico, where he could rest forever.

Once again, the dignitaries gathered, and a few of the faces would have been familiar to Smokey. Seldom has an animal of the wild been so honored. He had performed a great service for his fellow creatures, for the land, and for mankind. It has been estimated that the campaign initiated in Smokey's name has saved the United States more than ten billion dollars in timber, recreation area reconstruction, and watershed restoration.

Smokey was laid to rest among the trees of the Lincoln National Forest, but his memory will be carried on through the continuing campaigns to prevent forest fires. The children who came to know and to love Smokey after he survived the fire are adults now, but today's youngsters also know him. The children of future generations, through Smokey, will help to preserve the forests and all the wild creatures that live in them. I am proud to have played a small roles in the story of Smokey the Bear.

CHAPTER **15**

APPOINTMENT AS DIRECTOR

I WAS FIRST APPOINTED assistant director of the New Mexico Game and Fish Department in 1940 and held that position until 1953. Throughout my term I supervised trappers all over the state, moving them wherever predators, especially coyotes and mountain lions, were doing the most damage to livestock. But my primary responsibility was public relations work for the department. I attended Wildlife Conservation League meetings throughout the state, as well as meetings of the Izaak Walton League, which supports wildlife programs throughout the country. I also attended meetings of the National Wildlife Association and the Western Association of State Game and Fish Directors. I talked to the chapters of these organizations about the department's new programs in those areas of wildlife management that particularly concerned each organization. Many of these new programs were started in conjunction with the United States Fish and Wildlife Service, and included the purchasing of land and water rights. Often the department would buy worn-out homesteads in areas where game was suffering from lack of habitat and restore the habitat to support game. Sometimes the department would buy water rights from nonproductive farms and build a lake, which would be stocked with fish and surrounded with vegetation to provide good habitat for migratory birds. The state engineer's office assisted us in obtaining the water rights and the Game Department would construct the dams to form lakes for fishing.

The department also oversaw the transplanting of antelope from parts of the state where they were plentiful to those places with sufficient habitat where they were relatively scarce. We also traded antelope to Oklahoma, Colorado and Arizona for the native game they had that we needed (and had a sufficient habitat for) in New Mexico. In one case we gave Oklahoma a number of antelope in exchange for elk, which we transplanted in the Tres Piedras, Mount Taylor, and Gila areas. We also purchased elk by the truckload from the National Park Service at Yellowstone. In 1956 we transplanted sixty-six head of these elk near Los Alamos; they soon migrated up into the Valle Grande.

Another of my responsibilities as assistant director was to make movies of the department's activities. I presented these movies at the meetings of various wildlife associations. I edited and narrated them because the films at that time were silent. This kind of public relations work kept me quite busy lugging my projector around the state. Some of the movies were about transplanting wildlife; one featured a lion hunt in the Gila country; and one concerned our transplanting wild turkeys to Wyoming in exchange for sage grouse, which we planted between Taos and Tres Piedras in the sagebrush country. Yet another movie showed the transplanting of Gambel and Blue quail from one part of the state to another. These films focused on trapping techniques as well as the habitat into which the animals were introduced.

I was a one-man production crew for these movies. When the photography project was began, there was no one else in the department who even cared to deal with it. Since there were so few employees of the department, and since I enjoyed fooling with camera gadgetry, the lot fell to me.

Another of my responsibilities was to attend, with the director, the annual meetings of the Western Association of State Game and Fish Commissioners, which were held at different times in the eleven western public land states. I served as vice president of the association one year before I retired. I sat on several committees within the organization and worked with their financial and other problems. In 1978 I was given a plaque honoring me as a life member of the Western Association of

APPOINTMENT AS DIRECTOR

State Game and Fish Commissioners, and I am very proud of that award.

The New Mexico Fish and Game Commission is a five-man board appointed by the governor. Its members are appointed to staggered terms. When Elliott Barker reached the age of retirement in May 1953, the Commission appointed me his successor as director of the department.

Soon after I accepted the position I began to reorganize the department. New Mexico was behind many other states with regard to the employment of biologists to study wildlife habitat and behavior. With the revenue from hunting and fishing licenses, which at that time was good, I began hiring both biologists and additional district conservation officers. These people were necessary to further our studies and protection of our natural, renewable resources so that the greatest number of people could benefit from them.

I also restructured the department, establishing four districts within the state. The headquarters for these districts, which housed a director, several assistants, and one or more biologists, and game managers were Las Cruces, Albuquerque, Raton, and Roswell. This distribution allowed for more efficient response to local wildlife problems than had been possible when all administrative offices were located in Santa Fé. Another advantage of this setup was that game and fish information once only available in Santa Fé became more accessible at a local level. This system is still maintained in New Mexico, as it is in several other surrounding states.

During my term as director, the department began to receive more federal matching funds to expand many of the projects I had been involved in as assistant director during the years 1953-1958. The department was responsible for the creation of Clayton Lake, Snow Lake, and Fenton Lake. The Red River, Glenwood Springs, and Lisboa Springs fish hatcheries were improved and expanded with newly-purchased water rights.

When I assumed the directorship of the department, the state parks in New Mexico were all under our supervision. The public was demanding expanded park facilities at that time, and the burden of dealing with the state parks had grown too heavy for our department. Given the authority from the fish and game commission, I began to transfer park property and the administrative responsibility for it to the New Mexico State Park Commission, which had previously had no real control over maintenance of the parks. The new state park law then required the Highway Department chief and the Game and Fish director to serve on the Park Commission.

Through my assistant director, A. J. Garner, and other aides, we worked out a cooperative agreement with the New Mexico State University at Las Cruces, to set up a new program to provide a game management degree for interested students. It was to be taught in New Mexico to train graduate students in wildlife management who would then stay and work in the state. Up to that time, most of the qualified wildlife students we employed came from outside the state.

I hope that through these various construction, expansion, and reorganization programs I strengthened and streamlined the New Mexico Game and Fish Department during my term as director. It had been my aim to relieve the department of some of its excess responsibility and to bring its activities closer to the public it served. And I think to some extent I achieved those goals.

CHAPTER 16

MOUNTAIN LION TRAMPLES PEDESTRIAN

IT WAS LATE IN the night when I arrived at Roy Snyder's lion hunting camp at the Frank Dine Ranch, and Roy was sound asleep. He explained to me after I finally woke him up that he was very tired after a long ride that day up Diamond Peak Lookout on top of the Black Range Mountains to find some fresh lion tracks. Sometime ago Roy and I had planned to meet at the Frank Dine Ranch when Roy moved his camp to that location to make a new moving picture of a lion hunt. The game department had recently received several reports from ranchers living in the Winston and Hermosa country that the lions were plentiful and doing considerable damage to both game and livestock. Roy, a lion hunter for the New Mexico Game and Fish Department, had moved his camp a few days ago to this ranch and phoned me to come on down for the hunt. Frank Dine loved to lion hunt as well as I did and wanted to cut down the lion population on his allotment in the National Forest. It was a cinch that he would find time from his ranch work to hunt a few days with Roy and me.

Before we had settled down comfortably in our sleeping bags for the night, Bill Humphries from Truth or Consequences drove up in his car with his trailer and saddle horse, hoping to ride with us a few days. He set off an alarm among Roy's seven hounds that caused us to forget about the sleep we needed to be able to sit in a saddle all next day. We quickly ushered Bill to his sleeping bag with only a few bites of supper and a promise of a good breakfast of ham and eggs at four o'clock the next morning. Bill had never been on a lion hunt before, so he kept talking to me about what might happen tomorrow if we did find the tracks of a mountain lion. All of this chatter bothered Roy, so he called out, "If we don't hurry and get settled in bed and stop talking about what might happen tomorrow, we just might not have time to even brew a cup of java for breakfast, much less cook ham and eggs."

Early next morning we had just about finished washing the breakfast dishes when the dogs began barking as Frank Dine rode up, ready for the day's hunt. His home was only a short distance down the canyon from where we were staying. Frank was raising cattle on this northeast part of the Black Range and knew every trail and canyon up to the three lookout towers on top of the range. We were certainly glad that Frank could ride with us today, since we had decided to hunt the north and south Palomas Creeks where they head against the main range near Diamond Peak Lookout. All of the Black Range is rugged country, especially the east slope where the canyons head and flow down through deep gorges toward Elephant Buttte Lake.

I was riding Roy's pet saddle mule that day, but even that didn't keep me from getting sore "where the saddle met me" about four o'clock in the afternoon, still ten miles from camp. You see I just hadn't had the opportunity to ride horseback as much as I had several years before, when I was doing all the lion hunting for the department. Sitting in a cushioned swivel chair eight hours a day certainly had not kept my "saddle" ready to meet four o'clock on any afternoon!

We arrived back at camp about sunset without seeing any deer and only a few old lion scrapes. Male lions usually make the scrapes under pine trees in low saddles, on narrow ridges, or near rock ledges along their routes of travel. A hunter is thrilled when he finds these markers because he knows a lion has been in the country. There was no fussing around that night, because we were all tired; it was a little cloudy and rained just enough to help us enjoy our sleep.

The next morning Frank suggested that we ride south and west onto the Hermosa Ranch, since he had sent word to the manager, Mr. "Pecos" McFadden, that we would hunt on his range that day. Circle Seven and Morgan canyons cover a lot

MOUNTAIN LION
TRAMPLES PEDESTRIAN

of rough country and head just north of Reed Peak Lookout tower. To our surprise, while trying to rim across Circle Seven Canyon in the roughest part, we met Mr. McFadden in a place where only lion hunters meet. We had been rimming high on Brushy Mountain when it was decided that since we had not found much lion sign we would climb down through the bluffs to lower country. It was rough going, and we had to lead our horses through cracks in rocks and straight down where it was impossible to climb back up. Just then, the dogs barked down in the canyon, indicating maybe a lion or bobcat had been there, so we felt some better. It was still plenty dangerous sliding down over loose rocks and under brush where limbs would hang on the saddle horn and almost tear your saddle from the horse's back.

It was then we heard a voice down in the canyon yell, "Climb to your left around that ledge, and you can get your horses down into the canyon." Mr. McFadden had heard the dogs and gone to them and then heard us sliding over the rocks as we made our way slowly off the mountain toward them. The dogs had found some old lion scrapes that were not very fresh, but they could still trail them under trees and cliffs where the scent was protected.

Pecos McFadden had been on many lion hunts in Arizona several years ago before moving to New Mexico, and he, like Frank Dine, would always give up ranch work any day for a good lion hunt.

We started out to finish the day, since we were a long way from camp by now. Bill suggested that we had better head for camp, because the clouds were beginning to form heavy and black above us. But old lion hunters are like old soldiers, they never turn back. So we headed deeper into the rough canyons to find a mountain lion. Roy was still leading the way and we were south of Morgan Canyon when rain, sleet and snow began to come down. Everybody rushed for cover under cliffs and trees except me; I had remembered to tie a coat on my saddle that morning because the clouds didn't look good. I fared well, but the others got wet and cold; and of course I took a ribbin' from the boys for packing a slicker. Soon we had to give up the hunt and head back to the ranch, since it had rained out all fresh signs and would be dark again when we got in. No luck this day, and again it looked bad for the hunters.

On this expedition I had the added responsibility of getting some action pictures of lion hunting to complete the department's new lion film. Frank could not go the following day because he had some ranch work that just had to be done, and his wife Marg insisted that ranch work should come first. Frank suggested that we hunt south and east of his ranch on Brushy Mountain, because he had killed several lions on that mountain in the past and had seen fresh lion tracks recently.

Roy thought this was a good idea, so he took five of his best dogs along for this hunt. "Old Spot," his main lead dog, was eight years old and a top lion dog. The other four were younger dogs, two well-trained dogs and two untrained sons of Old Spot. The latter two had just begun their long training to prepare them to take the place of Old Spot. Roy said they would eventually make good lion dogs but right now were into everything and wanted to run anything that jumped. To correct this he snapped them close together by their collars with a short chain so they would have to go on the same side of trees and brush or crash together if they didn't.

As we climbed through the rims on the east side of Brushy Mountain, the two young dogs, King and Bum, opened up on a fresh track. Roy did not say a word until Old Spot went over and checked the scent where the young hounds were making a lot of noise. Old Spot looked back at Roy, and you could almost read the expression on his face: "These two young hounds are barking at something that does not pertain to lion hunting." Roy quickly called them off this trail, and as we traveled a few yards further we could plainly see the fresh tracks of a fox that had evidently been hunting for rats and rabbits around the rocky ledges.

As we worked our way down into a box canyon to get across to another part of Brushy Mountain, we found McFadden sitting on his horse, a real lion hunter ready for the hunt. Pecos said he came up the the trail from the Hermosa Ranch into this box canyon because he figured a good lion hunter would never miss hunting this canyon. In the past he had seen lion tracks right along the trail where we were now resting our horses.

We were unlucky again, not discovering even a lion track or scrape, so Pecos suggested that we hunt south over the lower points of Brushy and if we didn't strike anything by that time drop off in the canyon and go to his ranch for lunch and fresh horses.

After a good lunch and a little rest at the Hermosa Ranch, we changed to fresh saddle horses and headed out south of the ranch to the North Seco Canyon. Pecos McFadden pointed out to Roy and me as we rode across the main divide between Morgan Canyon and North Seco that back to the west was real lion country and in the past there had been lots of lion tracks seen on Lake Mountain. Near the dry lake at the top of the mountain there are high rim rocks and ledges that make a haven for mountain lions. Bill did not ride with us that afternoon since it was necessary for him to return to our camp at Frank Dine's place and bring back additional equipment and dog food. This supply run would save us several miles, and we could head out south the next morning, ready to search the country for photogenic mountain lions.

As we climbed out on the main divide leading to Lake Mountain, Roy had to take his saddle off and clean out a few sticks that had gotten under the saddle blanket. When he cinched his saddle again, he remarked that the old .30-.30 rifle that he always packed in the scabbard was still there and ready for anything that might happen during the rest of the afternoon. We saw two coyote tracks on the main divide and judged that since they were hunting so near the trail they must have had a den nearby.

We climbed on down into north Seco Canyon, and as we reached the bottom of the canyon we saw the road that the forest service had built the previous summer when they had the big McKnight forest fire at the head of the Seco Canyons. This road was built with bulldozers to get supplies and men over to fight this big forest fire, which burned so much of the wonderful country on top of the Black Range. North Seco Canyon was now running a beautiful stream of water—a scene quite different from those of the past two years. Most of these canyons had been practically dry during this period and both livestock and game had had a hard time getting by.

As we headed up the canyon west we noticed on the soft ground that two coyotes had been traveling the canyon bottom, and that several head of cattle had been using the canyon. A little further up the road we noticed under a yellow pine tree evidence that a flock of wild turkeys had been scratching in the pine needles only a few days before. About that time Roy noticed that Old Spot was out in the lead, some distance ahead of the other dogs—deeply interested in some kind of scent on the ground. He began to bark, and all the other dogs rushed to his side to see what he had found. By this time, Roy had trotted his horse up to the place where Old Spot first began barking, and sure enough it was a lion track. The lion was traveling south across the canyon, but the dogs could not trail it very well, since it was days old. By that time Pecos McFadden and I were down with Roy, leading our horses and examining tracks. Pretty soon Bum and Old Spot trotted over to where King, the other young dog, was working, and they all began to bark enthusiastically at some fresher scent. Roy led his horse to where they were and called to me, "I believe we have really found a couple of fresh tracks." I led my bronc saddle horse over, and sure enough there were five lion tracks going in a northwesterly direction toward Lake Mountain. Roy and I were both amazed, and we looked at Pecos while he sat on his horse nearby. He said, "See what I told you, that's where they are headed for again, Lake Mountain."

By this time the dogs were about all straightened out and trailing the tracks pretty well toward the stream of water in Seco Canyon. The dogs had some difficulties in trying to follow the tracks when they reached the water's edge, a lion always hates to get his feet wet. The lions had walked up and down the stream for several yards before they attempted to jump across or wade to the other side. Finally, after crossing the stream to the other side, the dogs got the tracks straightened out and headed west right on out of the canyon, up the steep oak brush hillside, among the ledges and rims. King and Bum were again out in the lead a little distance away and found where the tracks of one lion had crossed a cow trail. They misjudged his direction and figured he had gone up the cow trail instead of crossing it. They took off up this trail, leaving the rest of the dogs and us far behind. For a moment, we felt sure they had jumped something interesting, but after Old Spot checked the trail, Roy began to use some language that could not be printed here about those dogs straying off and guessing too much about what the lion had been doing. It took Roy about twenty minutes to climb this hill and finally get those two young dogs back down to where the other dogs were still working the lion tracks.

By this time the dogs were making good time following the tracks, but there were plenty of difficulties for them. Since there were an old female and four big yearling kittens traveling together, they made tracks all over the hillside, and it was very confusing to the dogs. It seemed that the female was traveling in the general direction of Lake Mountain, but the yearlings wanted to play and roam in all directions and then wind their fun up by coming back to their mother. All this confused the dogs, especially King and Bum, who liked to get off by themselves and work fast, getting into things that were not quite in keeping with good lion hunting practices. After another hour's work along this trail, the dogs found where a whiteface calf had been killed a couple of days before and almost completely eaten up by this family of lions. Only the head, feet and part of the hide were left. They were covered in a pile of oak leaves, sticks, and trash in the bottom of a little rough canyon that headed on the south side of Lake Mountain. Of course, when the dogs found this, there was plenty of confusion for them, because the country was covered with lion tracks going in every direction. After quite some time, the dogs got the right track headed away from the kill.

A short distance up the mountainside we could see a few

head of cattle watching us and one whiteface cow mooing constantly for her calf. Her swollen udder indicated that this was the mother of the calf killed by the lion family. As usual, Old Spot solved the problem and trailed the track out of the canyon up the hillside going toward the top of Lake Mountain. Pecos went on with the dogs while Roy and I checked carefully around the kill to find the trail where the lions had dragged the calf off into this little rough canyon. It was easy to follow this drag mark of blood back a hundred yards or so to the edge of an old dry lake bed, where we found the exact spot where the old lion had killed the calf. The cattle had evidently been resting under some juniper trees when this old hungry mother lion sneaked up and pounced on the calf and killed it without much effort. There was blood scattered around and several tufts of calf hair on the ends of broken juniper limbs where the calf had made its last effort to save itself from the powerful jaws of this big cat. Suddenly we heard Pecos yelling on top of the mountain for us to rush up that way. Roy quickly put his horse out in the lead, ripping through the oak brush among the rocks.

For some unknown reason, the cowboy at the ranch had given me a young sorrel horse that was a little bit spooky. Each time a dog barked too close to him, he would jump and kick at the dog. He was a stout horse and could pack a man straight up the hill, but he was a little bit fresh for me and my camera equipment. Although this horse was sure-footed, it had a bad habit of trying to go under low oak limbs that would just about break your knee. He would continue right up the hillside, leaving you about half pulled out of the saddle on a limb. When I finally met Roy at the top of the ridge Pecos was gone, but we could hear a faint bark of a dog in the distance. We followed Pecos' tracks east down the slope, and pretty soon we heard lots of dogs barking in all directions. When we located Pecos he was down in a steep box canyon yelling to us that he thought the dogs had one lion treed down there. But when we climbed off down to him, we discovered that the barking was coming from one of the young dogs that had gotten rimmed off from the main pack. By that time, the dog had gotten straightened out and was following the trail of the other

MOUNTAIN LION TRAMPLES PEDESTRIAN

dogs on over into the next rough canyon. We followed on over the hill in a mad rush, fighting brush and dodging limbs.

We could hear two dogs barking treed way down in a deep canyon far to the east of where we were. This canyon was rough where the dogs were, so we had to rim around to the east on another high ridge to get down to the dogs. While crossing this high ridge, we could hear the other dogs barking treed far to the south. We slid down through the rocks to the first dogs and sure enough Bruce and Drum were barking at the lion up in a low piñon tree.

I volunteered to stay there with these two dogs while Pecos and Roy went on down to the next deep canyon almost a mile away to see what the rest of the pack had treed. I was anxious to make some moving pictures of this lion while the two dogs tried their best to climb into the tree with the lion. But dark, low clouds were drifting in over the mountain, and it was so late in the afternoon that it was impossible to think of getting any colored pictures that day. Bruce, the white-spotted dog, repeatedly tried to climb this piñon tree up about halfway, hanging low to the branches, but he lost his balance and fell flat on the ground each time. When Bruce first climbed halfway up the tree the lion changed his position and climbed to the top, trying to get as far away from the dog as he possibly could. The lion didn't know, of course, that this was as far as the dog could climb before he lost his balance.

The clouds were beginning to get darker, and it was getting later all the time. I began to wonder what had happened to Roy and Pecos. About that time I heard a shot echo way down the canyon, and I knew that they had completed their mission and would be back in a short while. It seemed to me hours before they finally returned with the dogs and a nice-sized yearling lion weighing about fifty or sixty pounds. Even though it was late, Roy felt like we might shoot the foot of this young lion in this tree so he would jump out and give the two young dogs, Bum and King, another lesson in real lion chasing. It was agreed that I would hold my horse and the chain of the young dogs on the lower side under the tree while Roy took a shot at the lion, which would probably jump out of the tree on the lower side. Roy sat down, took pretty good aim, fired a shot, but he missed the lion clean. The bronc horse jumped and so did the dog that I was holding. Both of them just missed trampling me, although I was trying to keep on the high side of the commotion. Pecos was sitting on his horse up the hillside above Roy, watching the whole thing and laughing at what was happening to me. Roy fired another shot from his .30-.30 and again missed. King and the saddle horse both jumped again, but just missed me. They dragged me down the hill in the rocks a little farther. Then I heard Roy say, "I'll be damned."

I looked back up the hillside then and said, "What is the matter now?"

Roy said, "I don't have any more ammunition for my gun."

I felt like saying, "Why did you miss him in the first place, since you were only about thirty feet away?" But I didn't say that because I remembered having once run out of ammunition myself at a crucial time on a lion hunt in Frijoles Canyon. I knew exactly how Roy felt.

About that time Pecos spoke up and said, "Well I'll be darned, I have three .30-.30 shells in my chaps pocket that I've had in these old leather leggins for seven years." The three shells were badly corroded and did not look safe to fire, but we all brightened up and Roy said he was not afraid to try one of them at the lion. He also said that he was not going to shoot at the lion's foot this time, even though King and Bum needed more training; this time he was going to shoot at the big middle of the lion, because it was beginning to get dark. Roy sat down against the tree, took deliberate aim with him old rifle, and hit the lion a fatal shot, concluding that day's hunt.

That night when we met Bill Humphries back at the ranch he was disappointed that we had sent him away to do errands and caused him to miss out on the kill. He had never been on a hunt when a lion was killed. Early next morning Bill, Pecos, Roy, and I headed out to the south side of Lake Mountain, where the whiteface calf was killed by the lions two days before. Sure enough, when we arrived we discovered that the old mother lion and the other two yearlings had been back to the kill and had placed many more tracks all over the area looking for the two kittens which we had killed the evening before. They had moved the kill and chewed a little more on the feet and head. The sun was shining pretty hot that morning, and the dogs were having plenty of difficulties trying to work out the right track leading away from the kill to where the lions were probably resting among the rim rocks. Every direction that we traveled or circled around the kill there were lion tracks both big and small, and each time we got a track singled out, it would not go any distance until there would be one coming back toward the kill.

By noon we had begun to make great circles around the kill, and it was shortly after this that we did pick up the track on one of the yearlings going west off of Lake Mountain through a low saddle that indicated they might be heading toward the top of the Black Range Mountains. Since it was late in the day, the dogs were tired and were not making much progress on the lion track. We were a little disappointed because it was a small track; we wanted to catch the old female, because she would make the best lion pictures.

About the middle of the afternoon, when the sun was shining very hot on the rims on the west side of Lake Mountain, the dogs, after much work, finally jumped the lion out of the rims and off down the hillside. The race was on! This time we all stayed close behind the dogs until they crossed some steep canyon headers that we had to go around. Here they got away from us for a little while, but as we rimmed around this deep box canyon, we heard them on the far side barking as though they were very close to the lion. As we sat there on the horses, Bill said, "Look, there she goes up into a tree." It was the old female. She had jumped up on a big rock and then jumped to the low limbs of a big yellow pine tree on a steep oak brush hillside.

The country looked plenty rough to us from here, but it was always my duty, with the movie camera of course, to go the lower side of the tree while the others approached the tree from the higher side. I had trouble coming up from the lower side of the steep canyon, but I finally made it at about the right location below the tree and tied my mule. I pulled my chaps and jacket off and started to get the movie camera out of the saddle bags when all heck broke loose. For some unknown reason, the old lion jumped out of the tree and headed right back in the direction we had come from. Pecos was not interested in making pictures, so he had stayed on the ridge across the canyon. The lion scattered the brush as she crossed out of this rugged canyon and ran within a few feet of Pecos, surprising him and his horse. She hesitated a split second to look at him and then look back toward the dogs following her. Then she swished her tail and bounded back west through brush toward the top of the Black Range.

By that time I had gotten all of my paraphernalia replaced and pointed my mule up the steep slope to the rim where Roy was waiting for me. We were far behind the other boys, since they had taken off behind the dogs and were trying to keep as close in the race as they could. Roy and I had to take it slowly rimming out because we were packing all the camera equipment. Once on top, we could see a little dust rising way down the ridge where the boys were going in a gallop on their horses, and we could hear the dogs barking in the distance down in some more rough country. We could tell by the way the dogs were barking that they had again treed the old lion. This time she had taken refuge high in a big yellow pine tree and did not seem to be as nervous as she was in the other tree.

The weather conditions were favorable, so I prepared to get the action pictures that the department needed so badly to complete its lion picture. Just as I was ready, Roy fired a shot at the limb she was standing on. With a fierce look she jumped to the body of the tree I was standing against and came half way down toward me. She was facing right into the camera. At that moment Pecos hit her with a rock and she came right on down the tree, jumping about twenty feet to one side and scattering bark with her claws. The chase was on again. I had the camera going all this time.

As usual, Pecos and the boys followed close behind the dogs in the chase, and I was the last one because I had to get my paraphernalia back into the saddle bags. I had to follow their tracks over other ridges and down into a small canyon until I heard the dogs barking treed again. As I rode up, Roy remarked, "She's on that big limb fifty feet up the big yellow pine tree and in an ideal location for you to get your pictures." This time I got the camera set in a hurry, but she seemed pretty content to stay in the tree. We had difficulty persuading her to jump out of the tree so we could get those action pictures. Each time a shot was fired into the limb she was resting on she would jump another limb higher in the tree, refusing to come down the tree and face the dogs and camera again. I was as close as I could get under the tree to be in the right position to make motion pictures of everything that might happen.

There was a steep little canyon a few feet behind and below me and some big boulders to my right. I was facing the tree and holding the movie camera steady against my head, watching every move the lion made through the viewfinder. The other fellows were scattered around the tree on the steep hillside out of the way of the barking dogs. Suddenly everything broke loose. Roy took good aim at the lion and tried to fire the fatal shot, but missed the shoulders and hit the lion through the body. Hurt badly, she jumped off the big limb and sailed through the air, tumbling before she hit the ground. I watched all of this nervously through the viewfinder, as the camera clicked off sixty frames per second. She appeared to be about twenty feet away, but when she hit the ground I moved the camera away from my face and discovered the illusion. The next instant she trampled me and dashed down the canyon. I fell backward into the canyon, and seven hounds ran over me trying to catch the lioness.

My head had just missed a big boulder in the bottom of the canyon, but the bulky 16 mm camera, had smashed my hand against the rocks. I lay still for a moment. When I looked up I saw Roy. He was saying, "Are you hurt bad or can we pick you up?" Pecos and Bill arrived and tried to help me sit up. By that time I could talk but felt sick all over and had to lie back down. After a few minutes, I could think, so I told someone to go kill the lion before she got away again. I soon felt better and the boys began to chuckle about what had happened. Roy went down the canyon a few yards to where the dogs were baying the lion against the canyon wall and gave it the mercy shot. By that time I could walk around, and I wiped the blood from my hand and arm.

It was not until later that I could realize just what had happened and how badly I was hurt. I was bruised and bleeding mostly all over. The camera was smashed, and two lenses were broken. When I straddled my mule for the trip to the ranch I realized I had broken one of my ribs. We rode down the canyon and Roy led the way with the old lion tied behind his saddle. He called to me when the dogs barked at some fresh lion tracks, "We've killed three lions, but here is a fresh track of a large male, and there are two more kittens left on Lake Mountain. Don't you feel better now?" All I could say without hurting my rib was, "A pedestrian doesn't have a chance anymore, not even in the mountains!"

CHAPTER 17

RETIREMENT AND MORE TRACKS

EARLY in 1958, after five years as director of the New Mexico Game and Fish Department, I decided that because of my age and certain political considerations I should retire. I completed thirty years of employment with the state by working for five months with the New Mexico State Land Office, which manages the millions of acres of state-owned land.

After my retirement from state employment, I went to work for the Clinton P. Anderson Insurance Agency in Albuquerque. Senator Anderson had been a good friend since 1927. Although the job paid well, I was not fond of indoor work, and after two years I began to look for something in my familiar line of work.

In the spring of 1961 the Atomic Energy Commission at Los Alamos announced a job opening for a conservation specialist. I quickly applied and was appointed to the staff in July. I was in charge of natural resources, including wildlife, in Los Alamos county and was assigned to develop and administer a resource program for that area.

I no sooner got my family settled in Los Alamos than I had a big problem on my hands: deer were absolutely running over the atomic city, trampling and devouring vegetable gardens, damaging fruit trees and shrubs, and holding up traffic. Members of the local garden club complained to me especially about the deer's fondness for roses and new spring tulips.

The deer also posed a great traffic hazard. Security personnel patrolling the A. E. C. land collided with thirty or forty deer each year, and many of these accidents, not to mention those that occurred on public roads, resulted in serious injury to the drivers. Just before I arrived in Los Alamos, a light plane touching down at the city airport had collided with a deer.

To relieve these problems and also preserve the deer, I began a program of live trapping and transplanting that lasted over the next five years. We trapped only during the winter months to protect pregnant does and prevent suffocation in the hot crates. About half of the more than 500 deer trapped during this period were given to the New Mexico Game and Fish Department to be transplanted in the Pecos Valley near Roswell and Ft. Sumner, and also on the Navajo reservation; twenty deer were given to Los Alamos Scientific Laboratory, Health Research Division, for Cesium-137 studies and other testing; and many were transplanted to areas closer to Los Alamos. During the trapping seasons E. E. "Bud" Wingfield, Dr. L. M. Holland, and Dr. Donald Peterson assisted me in general experiments involving the use of immobilizing drugs. Twenty deer were used in the experiments, and the new Gallamine drug (sucostrin chloride) appeared to be the most desirable among several different drugs for this kind of work, although further research was of course necessary.

I was also responsible for maintaining the many roads and trails owned by the commission. Most of these had originally been constructed by the U. S. Forest Service, which turned over the land to the A. E. C. when the project began in 1942. When the snows came in early winter, our crew cleared the roads for families coming in to cut Christmas trees, and we continued to maintain the roads through the winter and summer. We also kept up redwood trail markers for hikers and horseback riders. In addition to these duties I monitored the issuing and use of woodcutting permits in the area and functioned as a game warden during the hunting season.

While working at Los Alamos I came to know James P. Dunnigan, a businessman from Abilene, Texas, who had bought the Baca location No. 1 from the Frank Bond estate in 1962. Dunnigan's property had its eastern boundary in common with the western boundary of Los Alamos County, so my work often brought me in contact with him. In 1969 I retired from Los

RETIREMENT AND MORE TRACKS

Alamos and my wife and I traveled all over the U. S. and part of Mexico in a travel trailer. Throughout the summer I had enjoyed good fishing everywhere I had gone and was doing the same in the fall at Yellowstone Park when I received a call from Dunnigan, who wanted me to return to the Baca Location and help manage the annual elk hunt on his land. It seems the elk population in the area had grown so large that the New Mexico Game and Fish Department had given Dunnigan permission to allow hunters on his land that season to kill as many bull elk as the guides saw fit, and he needed extra help with that hunt. I continued to work as game manager for the Baca Land and Cattle Company, not only directing these hunts in the fall, but also assisting in the fencing of experimental trout fishing plots along Jaramillo Creek, San Antonio Creek, and the East Fork of the Jemez, I also instructed ranch guests in the skills of trout fishing. These guests often preferred fishing in the experimental plots, where no grazing was allowed and the trout's natural habitat could flourish. On the 100,000 acres are streams teaming with brown and rainbow trout, and such big game as elk, deer, bear, and wild turkey are plentiful. This is surely some of the most beautiful country in the Jemez Mountains, and in recent years it has become an important energy area. Geothermal experiments have resulted in wells ready to produce unpolluted power for the Los Alamos area, and this power undoubtedly will become an important source elsewhere in future years.

Since September of 1969 I have worked several weeks each year at the New Mexico State Fair, in the security division. My responsibility has been to monitor the stable area and see that the 1400 or more race horses housed there each year are not disturbed. One of the great pleasures of working at the fair has been meeting and getting reacquainted with many of my friends and fellow workers from years past.

CHAPTER 18

GOLDEN WEDDING ANNIVERSARY

AS I COME TO the close of this book, I look back over the many years of dedicated work of my life—its thrills, spills, but through it all it was a most rewarding pleasure to me. Had I my life to live over again, I would choose the same life style. My wife, Edna, our four children, and I have had faith in God as our guiding light and have been blessed with health and happiness. In my work in conservation, I have made lifelong friends throughout New Mexico, and I cherish the memory of each of these special people in my life. Many of the friends I worked with in my early days in New Mexico have since passed on: Judge C. M. Botts, Ed Springer, George Turner, Judge Colin Neblett, G. W. "Dub" Evans, Senator Clinton P. Anderson, and Governor Clyde Tingley. Although none of them will be reading this book, all of them encouraged me to write about my experiences in New Mexico so that others could enjoy the stories they'd heard.

Over the many years I worked in the field of conservation, I traveled to every county in the state and met many people interested in our wildlife management programs. Our conservation programs were set up to provide the most benefits to the greatest number of people. Originally, this goal was realized by working with the Game Protective Association and the New Mexico Livestock Association and National Wildlife Federation. All were dedicated to the same cause: to conserve our renewable natural resources of soil, water, timber, and wildlife. My life has been dedicated to this ideal in the hope that future generations will continue to enjoy the great outdoors through the proper care and management of our renewable natural resources.

I am indebted to my loving wife, Edna, and to our four wonderful children for their patience over the years while this book was being prepared. I am so proud of them and their families: Col. Homer C. Pickens Jr. and his wife, Jo and their son, Homer III; Jack E. Pickens, his wife, Deanna, and their son, Jack Jr., and daughters, Cynthia and Jennifer; LTC. Jimmy B. Pickens, his wife, Joana, and their daughters Kathleen Pickens Grace and her husband, Michael, and their son Ryan Christian Grace and Danette Pickens Hooker and her husband, David Hooker: Betty Ann Pickens Cabber and her husband, Max Cabber Jr, and their sons Max III and Michael. Homer Jr. (Colonel, USA) and Jimmy (Lt. Colonel, USAF) were in fifteen campaigns in the Vietnam War. Jack served two years in the Air Force and now is a Staff Engineer with IBM. Betty Ann is a Training Supervisor with Mountain Bell Telephone Company. The successes of our children have been a source of great reward to Edna and me.

Our children and their families honored us with a wonderful reception for our fiftieth wedding anniversary, which was held at the Officer's Club at Kirtland AFB. Over 150 friends and relatives attended, and among the many letters, telegrams, and phone calls received, I quote from a few:

Mr. and Mrs. Homer C. Pickens

Annie, Andy, and Bryan join me in sending congratulations and every best wish on your fiftieth wedding anniversary. Your friendship is one of our proudest possessions. The Baca and the world are better places for you having graced them. Many happy returns.

    James P. "Pat" Dunigan, Abilene, Texas

Dear Homer and Edna,

We do want to congratulate both of you on your fruitful lives. My observations tell me that your lives are an example of family life at its best. I feel that there have existed in you throughout your lives great reservoirs of love and care which have been shared with each other, with your family, and with your friends. This is the true success.

    U.S. Federal Judge Santiago E. Campos, Santa Fé

Mr. and Mrs. Homer C. Pickens

God keeps you in your loving hours together and guides you by his light as he walks along your road and, best of all, to have that Abrahamic heritage that your children looking back will bless you and all you have touched will bless. Then you in turn will bless the Lord who gave you everything to enjoy.

    Arthur, Avonna, Lee, A. J. III, and
    Andrea Landwher, Evanston, Illinois

My concluding words for this book are, May we all find greener pastures as we grow older in this world and the world beyond.

HIGH-LONESOME BOOKS

"Published in the Greatest Country Out-of-Doors"

At **HIGH-LONESOME BOOKS** we have a great variety of titles for enthusiasts of the Southwest and the great Outdoors—new, used, and rare books of the following:

Southwest History

Wilderness Adventure

Natural History

Hunting

Sporting Dogs

Mountain Men

Fishing

Country Living

Environment

Our catalog is FREE for the asking. Write or call.

HIGH-LONESOME BOOKS
P. O. Box 878
Silver City, New Mexico
88062
575-388-3763
Orders@High-LonesomeBooks.com

Also, come visit our new bookshop in the country
at High-Lonesome Road near Silver City or on-line at
www.High-LonesomeBooks.com